K
Climbi

Jani Vaaranpaa
K. Hanna

Library and Archives Canada Cataloguing in Publication

Vaaranpaa, Jani, 1972-
        Kelowna rock : climbing and bouldering / Jani Vaaranpaa, K. Hanna.
Includes index.
ISBN 978-0-9697198-6-1
        1. Rock climbing--British Columbia--Kelowna Region--Guidebooks.
2. Kelowna Region (B.C.)--Guidebooks. I. Hanna, Karin, 1962- II. Title.

GV199.44.C22K43 2008   796.522'3097115   C2008-901076-0

Kelowna Rock
words: Jani and Hanna photos: Hanna maps: Jani Vaaranpaa route info: Jani Vaaranpaa
boulder info: Jani and Mike Shannon design: Hanna typesetting: Sally Foucher

Contributors
photography: Steve Jones, April Smith, Mike Shannon, Jani Vaaranpaa, John Lang, Barb Crawford
pilot: Tyler McNabb gear: Joan Clancy, John Lang and Clee Roy route setters: (pg. 45)
advisors: Kevin McLane, John Lang, Nicola Estrada, Janice McQuilkin proof: Nicola Estrada
Boulderfields signs: John Hoffer advertisers: (see pg.130) belayers: Thank you all.

Distributors
Blue Moose Publications, QuickDraw Publications
For the distributor in your area contact Hanna at: Blue Moose Publications bluemoo@telus.net

Front Cover: Jani on *From Start to Finish*, Lonely Boy Back Cover: Pentagon, the Boulderfields

Mixed Sources
Product group from well-managed
forests and other controlled sources
www.fsc.org Cert no. SW-COC-1271
© 1996 Forest Stewardship Council

FSC

*Printed in Canada on Garda Silk paper, which contains
FSC- certified wood fibre from well-managed forests. FSC
is the only forest certification standard supported by
organizations such as the World Wildlife Fund of Canada,
Sierra Club of Canada and Greenpeace.*

CONTENTS

Welcome to Kelowna Rock!

While there are several microcosyms of climbing near Kelowna, this guidebook focuses on the most developed areas - the Boulderfields, Cedar Park (including the Lair), the Lonely Crags and Mount Boucherie. Jani took care of route descriptions / grading and Hanna shot the photos (unless otherwise noted). If a route setter date is missing it is because (1) we were unable to contact the route setter or (2) memories get fuzzy after time. Every route has a corresponding photo and/or directions to its location. If you have information that we missed, or new information, please contact us.

Grading and Route Description

Controversy always exists over grading of routes and the style of write-ups. Grading in Kelowna Rock is based on climbing the route, comparing it to overall grading on the wall, and getting feedback from the route setter and its climbers.

Writeups are subjective, like a movie review, and even if you don't agree with the words, Jani has supplied a wealth of information for personal interpretation. For example, "a long reach" or "crimpy holds" or "burly roof" may up the suggested grade if you have short limbs, big hands or little muscles. Along with the grade, pay attention to number of bolts vs. length of the route, as well as the name of the setter. Each route-setter is an artist, and after a while you may choose climbs according to the attached signature (or cross it off your list of must-dos). Grading in Kelowna Rock is based on the Yosemite Decimal System (YDS).

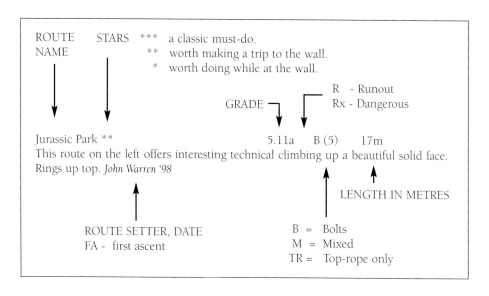

ROUTE   STARS   ***   a classic must-do.
NAME   **   worth making a trip to the wall.
                 *   worth doing while at the wall.

R - Runout
GRADE   Rx - Dangerous

Jurassic Park **   5.11a   B (5)   17m
This route on the left offers interesting technical climbing up a beautiful solid face. Rings up top. *John Warren '98*

LENGTH IN METRES

ROUTE SETTER, DATE
FA - first ascent

B = Bolts
M = Mixed
TR = Top-rope only

Conglomerate and Gneiss

If you are planning a trip to Smith or Spain, Mount Boucherie is the ideal place for getting familiar with volcanic rock conglomerate. According to the Kelowna Geology Committee, 60 million years ago the volcanic activity in this area led to the creation of Mount Boucherie. More recently (about 10,000 years ago), the Okanagan was under a big glacial lake. When it receded, Mount Boucherie was covered with gravel and sand. Groundwater percolating through this sediment left random smatterings of calcium and quartz, which became the cement for surface conglomerate. Over time, mildly acidic rainwater dissolved exposed calcium clumps and washed away the loose pockets of sand and gravel, leaving behind beautiful, climber-friendly hueco jugs.

The Lonely Crags, Cedar Park and Boulderfields are all made up of 2 billion-year-old Monashee Gneiss. Gneiss, pronounced "nice," is considered the oldest type of rock in British Columbia. Also known as Shuswap Rock, Monashee Gneiss was part of the granite Pre-Cambrian Shield that made up most of North America back in the day. Buried up to 40 kilometres deep, these rocks were exposed to intense heat. Mountain upheaval further messed with their original mineral elements, metamorphosing and ultimately branding the rock with its trademark beautiful multi-colour bands. This is the same kind of rock found in many North American climbing regions, including Skaha Bluffs (Penticton) and Joshua Tree National Park (California).

Hazards

Poison ivy and poisonous snakes are not issues in the Kelowna climbing regions. Our hazards involve the rugged terrain of the Boulderfields and dead trees from the 2003 Okanagan Mountain Park Fire (see page 74). Standing dead trees fall over in the wind (and at times when there is no wind at all). If a fallen dead tree is blocking the trail, feel free to move it. Standing dead trees can also throw bark at you on the rare windy day, so heads up. Don't forget to look down too, because rotten, burnt root systems sometimes create partially covered, evil ankle-twisting holes on or near hiking trails. Trails in the Boulderfields are designed for experienced hikers (see pg 11).

In the spring, check for ticks, and in the fall, be aware of sluggish, generally harmless wasps in the huecos (see page 120). Wear proper hiking shoes or boots in the Boulderfields (aint no walk in the park!) and protect yourself on hot, sunny days with hats and water. From May through September it is usually several degrees warmer against the rock than the official temperatures. Record temperatures happen frequently on our south facing walls.

Environment Canada Climate Normals - Kelowna 1971-2000

	May	June	July	Aug	Sept	October
Avg. Rainfall (cm.)	3.9	4.9	4.6	3.3	3.6	2.8
Avg. Temperature (°C.)	13.8	17.6	20.3	20.1	14.9	8.5
Record Temperatures (°C.)	33	37.5	40	40	33	26.5

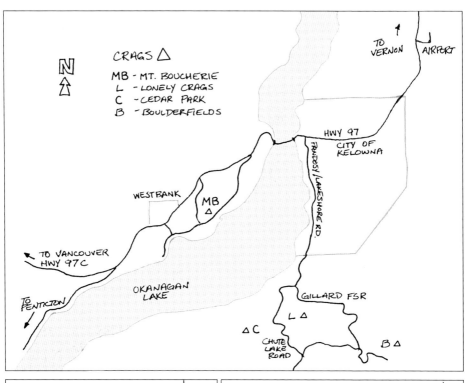

CRAGS △

MB - MT. BOUCHERIE
L - LONELY CRAGS
C - CEDAR PARK
B - BOULDERFIELDS

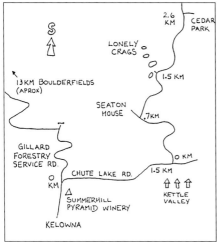

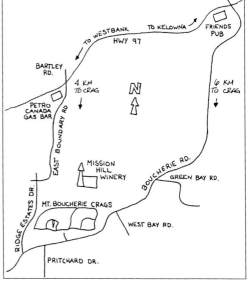

top: overview Kelowna crags, bottom left:
Chute Lake Road crags, bottom right: Mount
Boucherie (maps are not to scale)

Cedar Park, Lonely Crags and the Boulderfields

From Vancouver or Penticton (or points therein), take Highway 97N through Westbank, Lakeview and the Westbank First Nation. It is 15 km to Bennett Bridge from the 97c junction. Cross Lake Okanagan and turn right on Pandosy Street (south). From Alberta or Vernon (or points therein) continue on Highway 97S through town. Turn left on Pandosy Street. If you cross the bridge, you have gone too far. Good luck with that.

Carry on down Pandosy. At the Rose Ave intersection, you will pass the Kelowna General Hospital (on your right). At the KLO Road intersection, Pandosy changes to Lakeshore Drive. Keep driving down Lakeshore towards the Mission area of Kelowna. Continue past Sunshine Market (on your right) and the fruit packing house (on your left). The road climbs up to a set of lights at a three-way intersection. Go straight on Chute Lake Road. The roads winds left, up a steep hill. Near the top you will pass Summerhill Pyramid Winery (on right). It is 10.5 km from Highway 97 to the hill top.

The Boulderfields
At the top of the hill, Chute Lake Road levels out and swings right. You will go straight for 14.3 km. along the Gillard Forestry Service Road. (see page 8 for more directions.)

Lonely Crags
At the top of the hill, veer right for 1.5 km on Chute Lake Road, past the Gillard Forestry Rd. Drive through the Kettle Valley subdivision and turn left up the mountain, at the Chute Lake road sign. The road winds up the hill. At the fork for the Seaton House of Prayer, stay right, go around the curve, and park near the log house (page 6).

Cedar Park
Continue past Lonely Crags for 1 km. On your right will be a sign for Cedar Mountain Regional Park. Drive in and park.

Mount Boucherie

Mount Boucherie
From Kelowna drive on Hwy 97 South across the bridge. Turn left at Friends Pub (Boucherie Road). Follow Boucherie down to the lake past Green Bay Road and West Bay Road (approximately 6 minutes). Turn right into a small driveway with a utilities building. If you pass Pritchard Drive or Ridge Estates Drive you just missed it. Easy to spot Split Block when you turn around.

From Vancouver or Penticton (or points therein), take Highway 97N through Westbank, turning right at the Petro Canada station (Bartley Road). After passing Mt. Boucherie Secondary School the road veers right. At the stop sign, turn left on Ridge Estates Drive and then left again on Boucherie Road. Just after Pritchard Drive, the driveway for the crags will be on your left. Easy to spot Split Block.

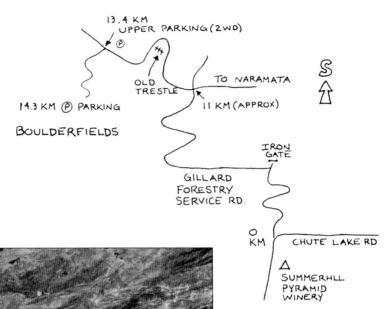

13.4 KM
UPPER PARKING (2WD)
Ⓟ

OLD
TRESTLE

TO NARAMATA

S
⇧

14.3 KM Ⓟ PARKING

11 KM (APPROX)

BOULDERFIELDS

IRON
GATE

GILLARD
FORESTRY
SERVICE RD.

O
KM
CHUTE LAKE RD

△
SUMMERHLL
PYRAMID
WINERY

KELOWNA

Once on Gillard, chances are about 100% that you will find the parking area. Park and head east (right) for 2 minutes along the fence line to the gate and signs. Don't make the same mistake as John Fantini and Kevin McLane on their first trip (pre-signs). After parking, they headed left into a disappointingly flat, climbless meadow. They weren't impressed!

left: Sonnie Trotter susses out potential boulder problems near Stepping Stone. (photo: April Smith)
facing page: Ben Hardin on the Cube.

8

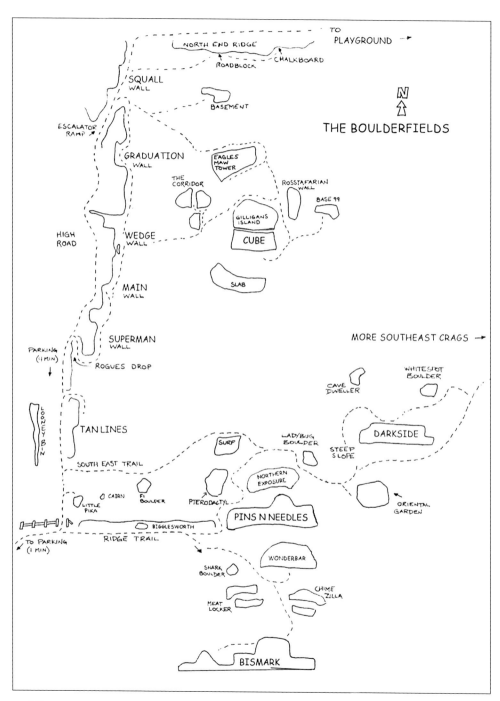

TO PLAYGROUND →

NORTH END RIDGE
ROADBLOCK CHALKBOARD

SQUALL WALL

BASEMENT

N ⇧

THE BOULDERFIELDS

ESCALATOR RAMP

GRADUATION WALL

EAGLES MAW TOWER

THE CORRIDOR

ROSSTAFARIAN WALL

BASE 99

GILLIGANS ISLAND

HIGH ROAD

WEDGE WALL

CUBE

SLAB

MAIN WALL

MORE SOUTHEAST CRAGS →

SUPERMAN WALL

WHITESPOT BOULDER

PARKING (¼ MIN)

ROGUES DROP

CAVE DWELLER

LOONEY BIN

TAN LINES

SURF

LADYBUG BOULDER

DARKSIDE

STEEP SLOPE

SOUTH EAST TRAIL

NORTHERN EXPOSURE

CAIRN

FI BOULDER

PTERODACTYL

ORIENTAL GARDEN

LITTLE PIKA

BIGGLESWORTH

PINS N NEEDLES

TO PARKING (1 MIN)

RIDGE TRAIL

WONDERBAR

SHARK BOULDER

CHIME ZILLA

MEAT LOCKER

BISMARK

10

The Boulderfields

Welcome to the ethereal experience of the Boulderfields, where there is more to the rock than nice Gneiss. It would appear that eons ago everything was good, everything was good, and then suddenly, BAM, this area just caved in like a sinkhole, creating a rim of climbing walls and a basin full of human-size to giant-size boulders.

Living hazards are few. There is no poison ivy or poisonous snakes to worry about. This is rugged terrain, however, particularly on the Southeast Trail and in the Centre Field area, so pay attention to your feet. Chasms and drop-offs are two good reasons to leave your dogs at home. If you get hurt or lost, call 911. Phone reception is a bit spotty but it exists. In the summer, bring lots of water and wear a hat.

While this is a sport climbing region, it is home to Natural Gas, arguably the best trad route in Kelowna. Nearby Devil's Elbow and Blumer's Bluff are being developed into trad / sport climbing regions, and will be included in the next edition of Kelowna Rock.

In fact, with the current explosion of development in the Boulderfields, all one can say is it is a work in progress. At press time, the Boulderfields had 32 developed walls, more than 140 climbs and numerous projects and problems on the go. As such many locals have stashes of 'gear' for quick access. This includes pry bars, ladders, pole brushes, ropes, stations and wire brushes. If you come across anything it has not been left or forgotten. Make no mistake: if you remove anything, you are stealing! The karma police WILL catch up with you and a fine will be imposed. Enough said. Enjoy yourself. Send!

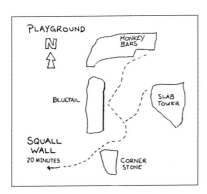

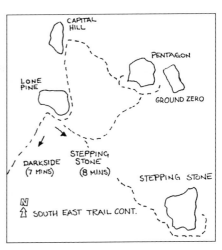

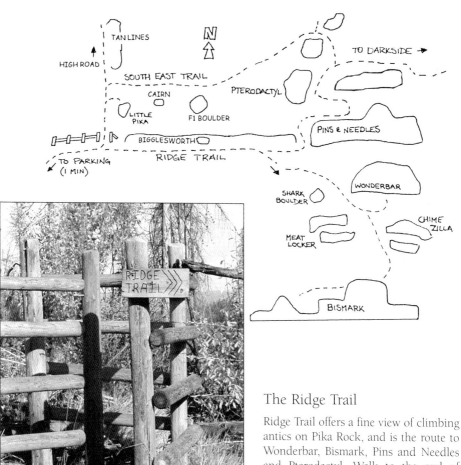

TAN LINES

HIGH ROAD

N

TO DARKSIDE →

SOUTH EAST TRAIL

PTERODACTYL

CAIRN

LITTLE PIKA

F1 BOULDER

PINS & NEEDLES

BIGGLESWORTH

TO PARKING (1 MIN)

RIDGE TRAIL

WONDERBAR

SHARK BOULDER

CHIME ZILLA

MEAT LOCKER

BISMARK

The Ridge Trail

Ridge Trail offers a fine view of climbing antics on Pika Rock, and is the route to Wonderbar, Bismark, Pins and Needles and Pterodactyl. Walk to the end of fence, and continue down the path marked by a sign post. Bismark is visible to your right as you walk along Ridge Trail. After about 3 minutes of walking the trail veers slightly right, and comes out at the east (right) end of Wonderbar. Bismark is 50 metres south of Wonderbar, and is accessed by scrambling between two boulders and walking through the undercut cave.

Pins and Needles / Pterodactyl is just below Ridge Trail. From the fence and sign post, walk about 2 minutes and to your left are cairns marking a chasm exit off the ridge. Carefully scramble down and stay hard right, to the base of Pins and Needles. The Pterodactyl is near the Pins and Needles cave. Alternatively, this area can be accessed via the Southeast Trail.

Wonderbar Wall is south facing, but gets some shade from a few mighty trees along its flank. Excellent for beginner climbers and leaders. Climbs can be set up on top-rope.

Wonderbar Wall

Exposure: south   Routes: left to right

The first three routes start down in a depression at the base of the crag.

1. Batman and Robin   5.8   B (6)   15m
Left side of the crag. The climb begins on a vertical brittle face, followed with a slab finish. Chains. *Tyler Parenteau, Adam Gant '96*

2. Giant Kubasa **   5.10a   B (6)   15m
Start 2m right of Batman and Robin. Interesting climbing up a nicely featured face. The intensity eases off, then one thin move. Quick links to rap. *Adam Gant, T. Parenteau '96*

3. Nonuts Needed *   5.9   B (6)   16m
Nice climbing on medium-sized crimps, with a big hold now and again. Slab finish. Hangers up top. *Adam Gant, Tyler Parenteau '96*

4. Copy Cat   5.9   B (4)   13m
Far right line on the wall. Move slightly up and left, then straight up to the hangers. *Tyler Parenteau '01*

Bismark

Bismark is the beautiful, north facing crag across from Wonderbar Wall. This crag gets little or no sun, so is a great place on scorching days. Short routes, but solid rock and fun to climb. Walking in, the 5.10a is above your head just after you exit the undercut.

Exposure: north   Routes: left to right.

1. Stiff Upper Lip   5.10b   B (3)   10m
Far left of Bismark area. The climb starts left of the huge undercut when approaching the next four climbs. This line was bolted and climbed just before press time. *Jeff Giebelhaus '07*

2. Face Value *   5.10a   B (4)   13m
The left-trending line of bolts. Start on the boulder platform and make a thought-provoking move on to the undercut face, with your belayer below and to your left. Climb the solid face on good holds to a nice finish. Chains. *Jani Vaaranpaa '06*

3. Your Story **   5.11b   B (4)   13m
A bouldery route up the right side of a blunt arete. Start 4m right of the last climb. A key starting hold no longer exists, upping the challenge to get off the ground. Crimp through a cruxy first bolt (Stick clip useful here!) to nice climbing on the arete and face. Rusty chains mark the end. *Todd Guy '98*

4. Shannon's Bald Spot   5.10b   B (4)   13m
The obvious line of weakness up an orange/brown wall, 3m right of the arete. Solid rock all the way up to a contrived finish. Chain / ring up top. *Jani Vaaranpaa '06*

5. The Bow **   5.13a/b B (5)   13m
The far right-hand line up the steep arete with fixed draws. Originally bolted by Todd Guy in '98 and done as a 5.12c (AO to the first draw). Sonnie came to town and dispatched the opening boulder problem (V7?) to free this longstanding line ground up. First 5.13 at the Fields! *FA Sonnie Trotter '07*

facing page and above: Sonnie Trotter soloing Shannon's Bald Spot, and then downclimbing it. (photos: April Smith, wall face Jani Vaaranpaa)

Pins & Needles

Exposure: north   Routes: left to right.

1. Jack in the Box   5.9   B (4)   15m
Around the corner from the cave is this uninteresting route on the scruffy east face.
No chains on the anchors. *Tyler Parenteau, Adam Gant '97*

2. Off the Couch ***   5.12b   B (5)   15m
The best 12b at the fields! Clip the draw on your left under the roof and climb straight
up. No show stoppers, but totally sustained. The proverbial redpoint crux awaits
below the fixed biners at the station. *Todd Guy '98*

3. Bewildered **   5.12c   B (5)   15m
Same start as Off the Couch. Start on the left side of the cave and climb under the
roof. Clip the draw on the right side and make some wild campus moves to join with
Keep Your Eye on the Prize. *Dean Urness '98 F.F.A. Todd Guy '98*

4. Keep Your Eye on the Prize **   5.12d   B (5)   15m
Stick clip the first bolt and make an unlikely first sequence to a reinforced hold (jug).
Shake it out and battle your way up to the station with fixed biners. *Todd Guy '98*

Pins and Needles is an excellent, challenging north facing crag with powerful bolted lines 5.10c to 5.12d.

5. Just for Jae *   5.10c   B (6)   18m
Found directly to the right of the 5.12 cave. Climb up the gentle slab past 3 bolts to the obvious vertical face at midheight. Good holds and clips to the crux and then the chains. *Dean Urness, Janelle Reimer '98*

6. The Crack   5.7   Trad   15m
This dirty crack was apparently ascended. *Adam Gant, Tyler Parenteau '97*

7. Burning at the Stake *   5.11c   B (6)   18m
Fun climb with a real puzzler under the small roof at midheight. Start 3m left of the large tree and tackle a smooth, white wall. Some suspect grips here (chipped?). Lower from chain and hanger. *Adam Gant, Tyler Parenteau '97*

8. Just Chip It **
        5.11d   B (4)   15m
Start on the large boulder and step left to clip first bolt. Climb straight up the arete and grapple with the non-existent features. A draining clip ensues, technical and powerful. Rap ring to descend. *Todd Guy '98*

Northern Exposure Crag

When approaching Pterodactyl there is a north facing crag to your right known as Northern Exposure, home to three uninspiring mixed routes. All three are dirty, with no chains. (no photo). Routes: left to right.

Tar Baby
        5.10-   M(3)   15m
Gary Penninga, Eric Penninga '98

Slippery News
        5.10   M(3)   15m
Eric Penninga, B. Labounty '98

Deadline
        5.10a   M(3)   12m
Eric Penninga, B. Labounty '98

left: Just Chip It, Pins and Needles
facing page: Rob Bannatyne getting
Off the Couch, Pins and Needles.
(photo: Jani Vaaranpaa)

8

Pterodactyl

The Pterodactyl is a good landmark and east facing for morning sun, with two fun technical lines 5.10+ and 5.11-.

Exposure: east   Routes: left to right

1. Jurassic Park **
        5.11a   B (5)   17m
This route on the left offers up interesting technical climbing on a beautiful solid face. Rings up top. *John Warren '98*

2. Tantric Tales *
        5.10c   B (4)   17m
Climb to the huge rail and hold your breath as you search for crimps to keep progressing. An interesting finish rewards you with rap rings. These two climbs really could have the grades reversed. *James Cruikshank '98*

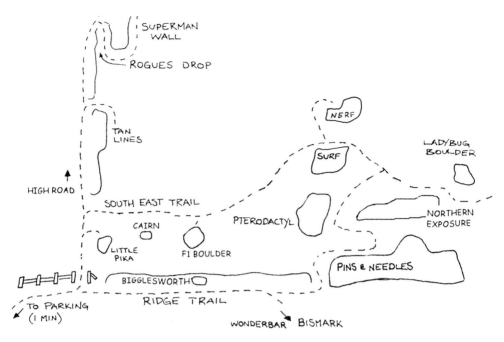

SUPERMAN WALL

ROGUES DROP

TAN LINES

NERF

SURF

LADYBUG BOULDER

HIGH ROAD

SOUTH EAST TRAIL

PTERODACTYL

NORTHERN EXPOSURE

CAIRN

LITTLE PIKA

F1 BOULDER

PINS & NEEDLES

BIGGLESWORTH

TO PARKING (1 MIN)

RIDGE TRAIL

WONDERBAR BISMARK

6

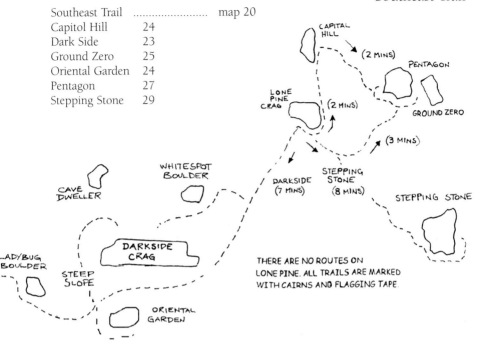

Southeast Trail

Follow the fence line north from the parking lot, and turn left through the gate. Almost immediately there is a sign directing you right, off High Road. The Southeast Trail takes you through scree and forest and big, blocky boulders. This Trail is the route to most of the currently developed bouldering problems (see bouldering, pages 63-73). After passing between Surf and Nerf, Pterodactyl / Pins and Needles can be accessed by taking the side trail to the right. Alternately, continue down the Southeast Trail. From here on in, pay attention to the flagging tape.

The Dark Side is about 15 minutes from the High Road. Hidden inside the forest, it is a quiet, cool, magical place to spend a hot summer day. Farther afield is the Pentagon and Stepping Stone areas, accessed by doing some low grade scrambling through the boulder patch. Pay attention to the cairns, and do NOT get nighted, as route-finding here in the dark takes on a whole new meaning. If you get hurt or lost, call 911. Phone reception is spotty.

The Southeast Trail is an exceptionally fun hike, but not safe for dogs.

Facing page: Sign man John Hoffer leading Dark Secret. (photos page 20-23 courtesy Steve Jones)

Dark Side

A tall, proud crag hidden from view in the forest (and hard to shoot!). The Dark Side offers compact, solid stone and is an ideal summer crag, as sunlight never hits the face. The approach from the parking lot takes 15 minutes; from Pterodactyl it is 7 minutes.

From Pterodactyl walk east along the trail into the woods. After about 2 minutes, to your right is a scruffy, bolted boulder (Oriental Garden) and a hillside of scree. Stay on the trail as it jogs left (north) and then right (east). Almost immediately there is flagging tape veering left into the dense woods. Follow the tape and after 1 minute there is a steep slope. Head down and left and then swing around right. Scramble to the base of the crag. Be careful on your approach in the spring and fall, as the beautiful moss-covered boulders are rather treacherous when wet.

Dark Side

All but Dark Secret start on the mossy ledge. Exposure: north Routes: left to right

1. Deception*   5.10d   B (6)   15m
Start at the far left of the crag in the smooth corner. The name says it all. Fancy foot-work and delicate moves get you past the crux. A lot of people end up sitting in their harnesses. *James Cruikshank '98*

2. Evil Intentions *   5.11c   B (6)   17m
Lead up obvious features. A tenuous move to gain a stance under the short roof, and then fingers of steel are required to pull over this one. Needs cleaning. *Jeff Giebelhaus '98*

3. Armed Robbery *   5.11d   B (8)   22m
A beautiful line of bolts leads to a short roof with a sharp corner feature. Once again, use your fingers of steel along with a high step to get on the face. Finish on the seam and progress to the chains way up there. Route needs cleaning. *Jeff Giebelhaus '98*

4. The Dark Dance *   5.11d   B (8)   22m
This one is a squeeze play but offers nice, thin face climbing. Start with the skinny seam. The real meat is halfway up and continues to the chains. *Jani Vaaranpaa '06*

5. Shady Deal ***   5.11a   B (9)   22m
Contender for best 11a at the Fields! This line starts on a black, rippled face and ends on the arete. Constant interest and a nice feeling of exposure make this a worthwhile journey. Chains. *Jeff Giebelhaus '98*

6. Dark Secret **   5.10a   B (5)   15m
A good warm up for the 5.11s. Scramble up obvious ramp and clip the first bolt. Engage the crack and enjoy constant interest all the way up. Face holds once in a while. Chains to lower. *Trad Ascent Tom Freebairn '98* (photo page 20).

right: Steve Jones on Shady Deal

Oriental Garden

This is the bolted, large boulder amidst the scree field you pass on the way to the Dark Side. Oriental Garden has 2 short problems bolted on the south face.

Routes: left to right.

1. Suki   5.10b   B(2)   8m
Tom Freebairn 97

2. Yaki   5.10b   B(2)   8m
Tom Freebairn '97

Capital Hill

Capital Hill offers a gently overhanging face on your way to the Pentagon.

Exposure: east

1. Capital Punishment **
                 5.11c   B (4)   10m
This awesome line starts off a large, white ledge. Trend up and left through a nicely featured face. Good incuts and underclings are the order of the day. Wee tiny chains.
Jeff Giebelhaus '02

In the centre of the U.S. Pentagon building there is an open courtyard known as Ground Zero. This is the only outdoor place in the States where soldiers are allowed to take off their hats and forget about the whole salute thing.

Ground Zero

This is the short, west facing crag directly across from Crack Addiction.

Exposure: west   Routes: left to right

1. No Salute *   5.10 c   B (4)   13m
Starts at the bottom of the slope off a stone platform. A thin layback leads to a rest below the smooth wall above. A little scruffy. *Jeff Giebelhaus '02*

2. No Cover *   5.10b   B (3)   12m
Scramble 3m up and right from last line. Straightforward climbing across a slight bulge will leave you searching for the hidden, finishing hold. A tad scruffy. *James Cruikshank '02*

Pentagon
south and east face

3   4   5

26

Pentagon

This is the crag to paint or draw or take its picture. The Pentagon is a large 20m high boulder with climbs on 3 sides. Beware of the route on the south side. There is good reason why the nice biner has never been claimed as booty. Routes: left to right.

West Face

1. Joint Ventures **   5.10b   B (6)   18m
Start at the bottom left side of an orange ramp with cracks. Scramble up and right to the vertical wall. Battle with the featured bulge up high, and lower from chains on top. This climb was created on lead by Jeff and Mike taking turns to get the bolting done. *Jeff Giebelhaus, Mike Ross '02*

2. Sideways *   5.11c   B (4)   18m
Easy scramble up the orange ramp to a good rest below the dark, blank face. Make a tough clip and keep searching for crimps and sidepulls to get you through to the top. Technical! *Mike Ross '02*

South Face

3. Loss of Equilibrium   5.12a   B (6)   18m
This climb starts around the corner from the last line. To date there has been a bail biner on the fifth bolt for 4+ years. Climb on right-trending features (easy 5.10) to engage the blank face above. Bad, bad landing if you miss the thin move. *Mike Ross '02*

East Face

4. Crack Addiction *   5.11c   B (7)   20m
Around the corner on the east facing aspect is this stunning line. Start down low in the corner, with your left hand in the obviously chipped hold. Battle your way through desperate moves to a small alcove (clip). Escape up and left to finish in the right-facing corner system. *Jeff Giebelhaus '02*

North Face

5. Project
Jani has started a promising new line on the arete right of Crack Addiction. *J. Vaaranpaa*

right: Jani prior to setting up the station on his north face project.

The Stepping Stone

The last crag on the Southeast Trail, 7 minutes past the Pentagon. Stepping Stone has some great routes with still more potential. Morning sun! Exposure: south   Routes: left to right

1. Spice of Life *   5.10b   B (4)   14m
Start up a featured face to a thin move below the right-facing corner. Stem your way up to the chains. Definitely worth a go. *Jeff Giebelhaus*

2. The Right Step *   5.8   B (5)   16m
Start on the arete with a long drop on your right (clip). Work your way up on big holds to 'the right step' up top. Good fun and view! *Mike Ross*

3. Skid Love *   5.13a   B (6)   16m
Starts far left side of Stepping Stone's main face, below the arete of The Right Step. Climb to the obvious roof above your head and clip a bolt. Boulder through the cruxy face using small holds and technical foot work. Eases up to 5.11- before the chains. Bolted by Craig Langford in '06 and as of press time only one ascent. *FA Ben Hardin '07*

4. Morning Stiffie **   5.11c   B (7)   20m
Start under a small roof, between the juniper bushes and the wall. Crimp your way up and crux over the roof to a welcome stance. Easier middle section, with a little unfinished business at the top. *Jeff Giebelhaus*

5. Rude Awakening *   5.11b   B (7)   18m
Walk on top of a boulder to a low bolt. Climb on great holds (5.10) to a stance under a small roof. Reach up, clip and engage the crimps for your rude awakening. *Mike Ross*

6. Blockade   Project   18m
Loose block! *Jani Vaaranpaa '06*

left: Sonnie Trotter sussing out bouldering near Nerf Boulder, on the Southeast Trail. (photo: April Smith)

29

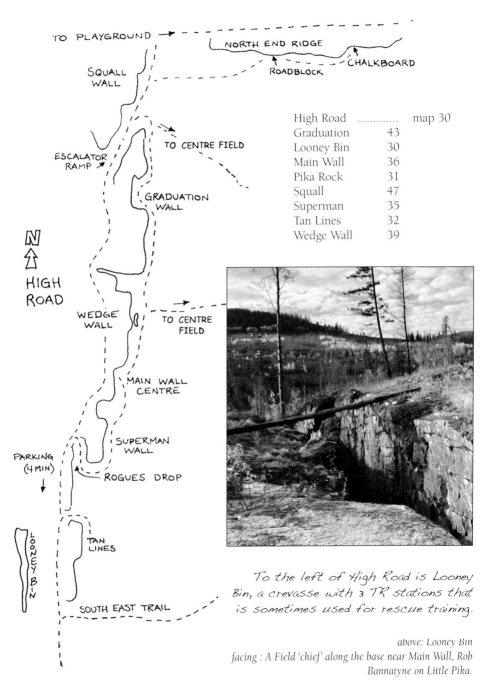

TO PLAYGROUND →

NORTH END RIDGE

ROADBLOCK

CHALKBOARD

SQUALL WALL

TO CENTRE FIELD

ESCALATOR RAMP ↗

GRADUATION WALL

N
↑
HIGH ROAD

WEDGE WALL

TO CENTRE FIELD

MAIN WALL CENTRE

SUPERMAN WALL

PARKING (4 MIN)

ROGUES DROP

LOONEY BIN

TAN LINES

SOUTH EAST TRAIL

To the left of High Road is Looney Bin, a crevasse with 3 TR stations that is sometimes used for rescue training.

above: Looney Bin
facing : A Field 'chief' along the base near Main Wall, Rob Bannatyne on Little Pika.

The High Road

The High Road follows the western ridge of the Fields, and offers great views of the Cube and the Centre Field. From the parking lot, follow the fence and turn left through the gate. To the right, there are 4 side trails leading down the ridge to the base of the crags. The less obvious trails to Pika Rock and Tan Lines are marked by cairns. The Rogues Drop exit is just 5 minutes past Tan Lines, and the Escalator Ramp is the

natural down-trending trail at the end of the Road. Alternatively, access the base of the walls with a full 30m rappel off Main Wall (tie a knot).

Pika Rock

Pika Rock is 20m past the gate, just before the Southeast Trail and Tan Lines. Scramble down and right to its very steep arete.

Little Pika **
5.11c   B (4)   10m
A sustained boulder line up and right. Flashed by John Lang for the FA! *Jani Vaaranpaa, Brian Gibbons '07*

Tan Lines

A great east facing crag 30 metres long and about 5 minutes from the parking lot. Grades range from 5.10b to 5.11c. Overall the rock is solid with some choss on the fringes. Follow the fence from the parking lot and go left through the gate. Just past the Southeast Trail is a cairn-marked trail. Walk down the marked path that veers right and in a minute you are at Tan Lines. Exposure: east   Routes: left to right

1. Giant Kauk *   5.10d   B (4)   13m
Far left side of crag. Scramble up and left on an ugly, chossy ramp. Clip a bolt and head up the nicely featured face to a big ledge / cave formation. Pull through to the jugs beside the station. Chains. *Adam Gant, Tyler Parenteau '98*

2. Summary Offence **   5.11b   B (3)   17m
About 2 metres right of last line, start beside the chossy ramp and climb to a bolt on the bulge. Carry on, straight up on technical holds. Watch for a big whipper on the way to last bolt. *Tyler Parenteau, Adam Gant '97*

3. Jolt *   5.10d   B (5)   18m
Start up the crack in the middle of the crag. Break left at the third bolt for a one-move wonder crux. Chains. *Tyler Parenteau, Adam Gant '97*

4. Teenage Tan **   5.10b   B (5)   18m
Start up same crack as Jolt. Nice moves on face holds, with a jam or two as you go along. For trad fans, note the really good gear placements as you head up and right. Chains. *Trad ascent, Geoff Atkins '94*

5. No Ethics, No Class   5.11c   B (4)   18m
This line starts 2m right of the crack with a bolt on top of the big, white bulge. Make the awkward mantle and climb into groundfall territory before clipping the second bolt. No chains on station. *Gary Penninga '97*

6. High Grade ***   5.11a   B (5)   18m
Another contender for best 11a. Climb up and right around a big chossy horn feature which sticks out from crag. Traverse left over the smooth white bulge and up on jugs to a super cool crux at 2/3 height. Chains. *Jeff Giebelhaus'98*

7. Melanoma *   5.11b   B (5)   18m
Easy climbing to second bolt. One thin powerful crux leads to jugs at the roof. Stiff for low eleven climbing. Chains to lower. *Mike Ross '98*

34

Superman

Approach by continuing along the High Road for about 200m past the trail for Tan Lines. The view of the Boulderfields opens up, with the Cube as the centre point. Scramble down Rogues Drop, the vertical chimney that takes you to the base of the crag. Just left is Superman Wall.

Exposure: east   Routes: left to right

1. Brutality ***   5.11c   B (6)   17m
Start on the large ledge in the middle of the steep, smooth wall. A low bolt allows you to move up and left on big, slopy holds. Climb to the horizontal break at 2/3 height for a rest, then deal with the right-trending crack to finish. The name makes sense when you clip the chains to lower. *Mike Ross '98*

2. Gorilla Grip **   5.12b   B (5)   17m
Start just left of the blunt white arete. A long reach gets you established on the steep face. Boulder on up using big but disappointing holds to a blank white face (crux). Finish on the ever steepening headwall. Chains. *Bolted by Todd '98. FA J. Vaaranpaa '06*

3. Rat's Ass   5.10b   B (4)   17m
This uninspiring line can be found around the corner on a separate belay ledge. Right-facing corner. *Marty Zikmund '98*

4. Griptonite ***   5.11b   B (7)   18m
Start 4m right of the corner on the exposed ledge. Climb up the rounded crack to the horizontal break for a rest. Great incuts lead you up the steep, brown wall to a surprise crux in the notch up high. Bolted by Jeff in the winter with the help of a ski-doo. Chains to lower. *Jeff Giebelhaus '98*

5 Battling the Bulge **   5.10a   B (6)   18m
This climb starts down and right from Griptonite on the face of a right-trending ramp. Delicate moves on good but rounded holds lead you to a runout near the top. Really fun climbing and nice exposure. Chains. *Mike Ross '98*

" *Griptonite was tough. I did it in the wintertime – snowmobiled up there by myself, and got stuck underneath the overhang. Took half an hour to get out of that mess!" JG*

facing page: Look carefully and you will see John Hoffer belaying
Steve Jones on the run-out Edgefest, Main Wall.

Main Wall

The next eight climbs are on Main Wall, a great place for setting up nice, long top-ropes. The first two climbs share the same station and go halfway up the 30+m high crag. At the far end of the Main Wall, there is a big left-facing roof where the crag drops down and right, heading towards Wedge Wall. Exposure: east   Routes: left to right.

1. Side Saddle *   5.10a   B (5)   17m
This climb is reached by scrambling down two ledges from Superman Wall (below fixed rope). A nice line which trends up and right to a station below a tree on a ledge. *Unknown*

2. Rope on a Tree **   5.10b   B (5)   17m
Start 2m right of Side Saddle, on the same ledge. Technical climbing to a ledge at mid-height where a high bolt ups the ante. Same station as last climb. *Marty Zikmund '99*

3. Edgefest **   5.8   B (6)   30m
Start at the right end of the ledge where there is a belay bolt. This baby is run-out and heads straight up to the top of the crag. Hold your breath as you pull gently on the suspect flakes. Easy to top-rope / rappel. *Marty Zikmund '98*

4. Route Canal **   5.9   B (11)   34m

A great moderate addition to Main Wall. Start below and just right of the ledge. Climb up to the ramp and straight past a left-facing feature. A consistent climb at the grade, with intelligent bolt placements. Can be climbed with a 60m rope if you lower climber to the belay ledge for Edgefest. Shares a station with Sweet Tooth on the right. *Jeff Giebelhaus '07*

5. Sweet Tooth   5.10a   B (8)   30m

This is the obvious left-trending scrub line which crosses the centre of the crag. Sweet Tooth is a bolting nightmare that Jeff G. has Terry's OK to fix. Lower from Route Canal station. *Terry Serhan '97*

6. Just Another Day *   5.10a   B (8)   28m

Originally done as a mixed line with two bolts. Now retro-bolted and a little runout for the 5.10a leader. Trends up and slightly right, with consistent climbing for the grade. The bolts seem to be where you need them, but watch for potential groundfall when approaching the third bolt. Chains. *Ron Collins '95*

7. Curt's Corner   5.10-   Trad   28m

This hardly repeated line starts just left of the broken corners near the big roof and finishes with no station. *Jeff Giebelhaus '97*

Main Wall cont.

8. Rachit   5.10a   B (6)   26m
Standing on the scree slope below the big roof, look up and you will see the Rachit
line of bolts on a face just left of the corner. An ugly start on blocks and through
bushes leads you to the high first bolt. Clip and finish in the left-facing book above.
Poorly bolted. Chains to lower. *Terry Serhan '97*

9. Field of Dreams *   5.10b   B (7)   22m
A fun, adventurous climb which suffers from an awkward approach. When standing
below the big roof, traverse along a loose, scary ledge towards a big pine tree. Thin
moves down low change to easier climbing all the way to the top of the crag. Chains.
Jeff Giebelhaus '98

*Note the route above tree on the ledge is the top half of Field of Dreams.
This route has a difficult, awkward approach.*

Wedge Wall

Follow the scree trail north from Main Wall. Wedge Wall is host to some of the best and longest climbs at the fields. The first two climbs are directly below Field of Dreams. They start left of a narrow wedge-shaped corridor that runs between a thick flake and the wall. The remaining routes are reached by squeezing through the wedge to a 3m wide ledge at the base of the crag. Wedge Wall continues down to the big white wall and the prominent, dual aretes. Exposure: east   Routes: left to right.

1. Wet Dreams **   5.10c   B (4)   17m
Left-hand line which leads to the large ledge with a big tree. Gingerly climb up to the second clip and then bring on the fancy footwork to get through the technical crux. Nice climb. *Jeff Giebelhaus '98*

2. Slanted Reality **   5.10c   B (5)   17m
Start left of the corridor. Follow the devious shallow seam up and left. Expect constant interest until you arrive at the station below the tree. Chains. *Paul Gaucher '98*

3. Snit *   5.11b   B (7)   20m
First line of bolts once you squeeze through the corridor. It gets right in your face from the opening sequence, until you are past the fourth clip. This line is edgy and full on! Traverse right and over the small roof. Chains. *Tyler Parenteau, Adam Gant '97*

These next two lines start together and are located about 3 metres left of the tall arete

4. No Retreating Footsteps **   5.12a   B (9)   20m
Follow a devious path along 3 close bolts to a knob, then go for the spaced out fourth bolt. The climb eases off until you get to the right-trending corner. Pull out for a blank finish. Chains. *Craig Langford '07*

5. Preuve Morceau   5.11c   B (11)   25m
Same start as last but head straight up at the top of the first feature. A series of nice moves leads to a vandalized white wall with an ugly, drilled pocket. This long and interesting line requires endurance. Chains up top. *Adam Gant, Tyler Parenteau '97*

6. 9-Minute Holiday ***   5.11d   B (10)   26m
The proud, rounded arete at the right end of the Wedge Wall. Start at the bottom of the tree and scramble up and right to the first bolt. Clip in and head for the arete. Great exposure and balancing moves make this a demanding line. Good protection. Chains. *Todd Guy '98*

7. Natural Gas ***   5.10+   Trad   35 m
The spectacular right-facing corner crack. Best trad line in Kelowna! Really good gear on a steep and committing line. Two bolts added to the face up top before the rap rings. The rack: nuts / cams up to #3 Camalot/ long slings. Can be done with a 60 metre rope if you start at the belay bolt for The Lost Boys. *Jeff Giebelhaus '90*

The next three routes are on the proud, white wall hemmed in by the crack at your left and the big chimney to the right.

8. The Lost Boys ***   5.11c   B (13)   30m
Scramble up and left on to some blocks with a belay bolt. A nice long journey up, with a left exit move over the roof. Three "lost boys" worked on cleaning and bolting this beautiful face climb. Chains. *Jani Vaaranpaa '07*

9. Janelle's Song **   10.d / 5.11b   B (8+4)   31m
Climb up to a ledge and a technical looking right-facing corner. Interesting, bold climbing leads to a station below the roof (5.10d), or carry on up and over the roof for the full 11b treatment. Use the midstation to lower. *Dean Urness, Janelle Reimer '98*

10. Lucifer's Lullaby *   5.12a   B (13)   35m
Route just left of the big chimney. A ferocious start with crimps, thumb jams and fading feet lead to easier climbing towards the roof. The next crux is pulling the roof. Nicely bolted line. There is some discussion about the grade. *Mike Ross '00*

11. Cool World
       5.9   Trad   30 m
The big chimney right of Lucifer's
Lullabye. A protectable crack exists
inside the chimney. This route doesn't
see much action for obvious reasons.
Lower off Lonesome Jubilee station.
Ron Collins '96

*As of press time, Craig Langford
was working on a new line between
Cool World (crack) and Lonesome
Jubilee (the arete). It will climb
straight up the face to the chains
up high (circled). The addition of
his first bolt will allow much
safer access to Lonesome Jubilee.
That's Jani on Lucifer's Lullaby
with Brian Gibbons on belay.*

Skaha has rattlesnakes. We have the American Pika,
a unique alpine critter living amongst the boulders
and talus blocks of the Boulderfields. You are more likely to hear the distinct 'eep, eep'
of these elusive critters than you are to see them. The pika is round, furry and about
15 centimetres (6 inches) long. They look like guinea pigs, but are actually related to
the rabbit family. Pikas do not hibernate, but live in snow tunnel systems during the
winter. Pikas do not perspire or pant, so excessive body heat is lethal ... which makes
you wonder why the Boulderfields with its hot, summer days is their natural habitat.

left: South end of Graduation Wall. facing page: Escalator Ramp, the easy trail down to the base level of the Fields. Grad Wall is below the Ramp.

① ② ③ ④

Graduation Wall

Just past Wedge Wall, Graduation Wall is host to several good quality routes. Extends from the arete of Lonesome Jubilee to a large, loose chimney. The crag has two sectors. The left (south end) is a solid white wall which is 40 meters in height at its peak. The right (north end) begins around the corner from the white wall. The climbs on the north end are especially good, with fun moves on a gently overhanging face. Overall rock quality is good on nicely featured stone.

Exposure: east   Routes: left to right.

1. Lonesome Jubilee   5.10d   B (10)   30 m
This is the left-facing arete with a tree at its base. Unfortunately this lovely arete is mis-bolted, run-out and scary. Another route that does not see many ascents for all of the above reasons. Chains up top. *Dean Urness, David Urness '96*

2. Body Language *
         5.11b   B (10)   28 m
Leave Wedge Wall and walk down the slope to the base of a tall, white wall. The start is about 4 meters right of the arete. Climb a short face to a ledge, then head straight up to the obvious undercling / overlap. Some strange body tension crux moves lead to fun jug-hauling all the way to the station. *Jani Vaaranpaa '07*

3. Test Driven by NATO
         5.10a   B (10)   25 m
Start at the base of the right-trending overlap, then climb along the right side of a big chimney. A disappointing line that needs to be retro-bolted. Chains to lower. *B. Labounty '97*

4. The Graduate *
         5.11c   B (15)   35 m
A long journey which starts on the featured wall just before the slope heads up and right. Two bolts lead to the cruxy bulge / overlap. Climb the slab to a very steep finish way, way up there. *Craig Langford '07*

The next 6 routes start left of the corner and go just past midheight of the crag.

5. Naked Obsession ***   5.12a   B (6)   18m
This route has the most solid stone on Grad Wall. Sustained climbing on big but slopy holds leads to a good rest and 'big move' crux. Not to be missed! Chains. *Tyler Parenteau, Adam Gant '97*

6. Valedictorian *   5.11d   B (7)   24 m
Devious, open-handed, slopy climbing on a featured face leads to a lesser-angled, crimpy headwall for the finish. this line is a bit tougher than its neighbor to the right. *Tyler Parenteau '97*

facing page: Craig Langford on Naked Obsession

Naked Obsession was the scene of a 15m groundfall when a loose block came off and cut the climber's rope. The loss of the block changed the route grade from 11c to 12a and a bolt was moved at the crux. Good and solid now. Amazingly, the climber hiked out - broken bones and all! - with help from his belayer.

7. Passing Grade **   5.11d   B (6)   20m
Dynamic climbing on big, open-handed holds with some good rests leads to a steep, crimpy, tan headwall. Gets a little bit sandy with run-off from the top of the crag, but still a really fun climb. Chains. *Adam Gant, Tyler Parenteau '97*

8. Frat Party *   5.12b   B (7)   20m
A squeeze play. Muddle your way through the start until the line is independent, then head for the obvious cruxy, tan headwall. The last bolt seems a bit useless where it is. Fixed station to lower. *Craig Langford '07*

9. Power Struggle **
          5.11a   B (8)   20m
Far right side of the crag. Climb on big, open hand slopers up to the fun, right-facing book just past midheight. Cool hand sequences and stemming lead through the book to a great exit move. Chains are up and out of sight. Like Passing Grade, it too gets a little sandy from run-off. *Jeff Giebelhaus '00*

10. Alien Intervention
          5.11d   B (9)   20m
The last line of bolts to ascend the tan-coloured face before the crag peters out. Technical face climbing leads to a steepening wall before the station. A bit scruffy like its neighbours. *Craig Langford, Rob Bannatyne '07*

Rob Bannatyne, Passing Grade, Graduation Wall

Squall Wall

Squall Wall is at the northern end of the Fields. From the parking lot, follow the fence and turn left through the gate. Walk along the High Road for 5 minutes and hop over a chasm (or take an easy left detour along solid ground). The path heads down Escalator Ramp, along a narrow trail that hugs the wall.

Squall Wall is generally not as solid as the rest of the big walls, but does have a few exceptions. The wall is divided into three sectors separated with distinct corners. The first sector is still on the sloping ramp and has one route (Find a Way – good luck). At the bottom of the ramp is an arete, and the beginning of the second sector which hosts 5 climbs. Another corner appears, followed by the last 3 routes. After Buddha Bulge, the crag disappears into a forested gully. Follow the gully for about 5 minutes and you'll hit the Northern Perimeter crag. Squall Wall is also where the trail to the Playground begins. That trail crosses the gully and heads to the cairns along the north ridge.

Squall Wall saw most of its development in the summer of 1998. On one particularly busy day, veteran climber Leon Blumer hiked in for a visit with the route setters. While not unusual to see the septuagenarian in the Fields, that day was a bit surprising as Leon was sporting a full leg cast.

Jani and John Lang
trying to Find a Way ...

Squall Wall

Exposure: east   Routes: left to right.

1. Find A Way   5.10b   B (7)   20m
Start near the bottom of the ramp, just right of a clean arete. The real challenge is getting off the ground and established on the wall. Chains to lower. *Paul Goucher '98*

2. Orange Appeal *   5.10b   B (6)   20m
Located at the bottom of the ramp, Orange Appeal is on the face just right of the second arete. Edgy face climbing with some really hollow and loose flakes along the way. Climbs well, but flakes are a cause for concern. Chains. *Jeff Giebelhaus '98*

3. Sweet Spot *   5.10b   B (6)   20m
Start 2 m right of Orange Appeal and climb on loose, flaky holds up to a left-facing feature. Bolts are a bit spaced out. Can be climbed on gear. Chains. *Marty Zikmund '93*

4. Oxygen Deficiency   5.10c   B (8)   20 m
This variation route has the same start as Sweet Spot. Move right at the second bolt and use face holds to follow the thin seam. Chains. *Jeff Giebelhaus '00*

5. Triathlon **   5.11b   B (7)   24 m
This well-named, easily identified route holds the best and most solid stone on Squall Wall! Climb the face with 3 bolts to a ledge, then another short headwall with 2 bolts to a ledge, then a final push to the station. Great finishing crux below the chains. *Mike Ross '00*

6. Lil Devil *   5.10c   B (3)   10 m
Lil Devil is found 3m right of Triathlon on a short technical face. Really good stone leads you up on disappointing holds to a route-finding crux. Chains. *Jeff Giebelhaus '00*

7. A Dirty Little Route   5.9   B (3)   13m
This route starts just right of the arete. Solo to the high first bolt and carry on up this face climb on solid edges. Chains up top. *Tom Freebairn '98*

8. Flower Power   5.10a   B (5)   18m
Starts 20 m right of last route in a slight concave section of the wall. Straightforward climbing leads to an odd runout between the third and fourth bolt, then finishes up with good stone on the spotless bulge. Quick links to rap. *Tyler Parenteau, Bruce Fairley '99*

9. Buddha Bulge   5.10d   B (4)   14m
This neglected route is at the end of Squall Wall and is in dire need of some TLC. Starts 20m right of Flower Power on a bulgy slab with some slimey, moss-covered horizontal seams. Best to be avoided. *James Cruikshank '98*

SQUALL

NORTH END RIDGE

ROADBLOCK

CHALKBOARD

BASEMENT

N

CENTRE FIELD

ESCALATOR / HIGH ROAD

EAGLES MAW TOWER

THE CORRIDOR

ROSSTAFARIAN WALL

BASE 99

GILLIGANS ISLAND

WEDGE

THE CUBE

Kevin McLane on 64th Parallel, Eagle's Maw

Eagle's Maw Tower

Eagle's Maw Tower is actually a very large boulder with a unique little point on top. Located just 3 minutes northwest from the Cube, it is the first crag on the trail from Escalator Ramp to the Centre Field. Eagle's Maw can be top-roped by walking up ramp on the right. Routes: left to right

North Face (no photo)

1. Executive Decision   5.12c   B (9)   20m

Stiff moves off the deck lead to a horizontal break and a welcome rest. Thin, technical moves just left of the seam take you all the way to the station. The grade and number of stars on this one is an ongoing debate. *Tyler Parenteau, Adam Gant '98*

2. Craig Langford has started a project to the right of Executive Decision.

South Face

3. 64th Parallel *
         5.10c   B (5)   16m
Start up the left arete and gradually trend right on to the face. A tricky crux welcomes you at 2/3 height. Route shares a station with Exhibit A. No chains. *Tyler Parenteau, Adam Gant '98*

4. Exhibit A *
         5.11b   B (5)   16m
Long moves on positive rails gets you going. Another hard-to-read crux leads you up and over the small, right-facing feature. Joins with 64th Parallel at the hangers. *Tyler Parenteau, Adam Gant '98*

5. Dead Short *
         5.10d   B (5)   16m
Far right line. A long, hard pull off a less than welcoming hold establishes you on the crimpy face. Thin moves follow to the obvious undercling and finale. No chains. *Adam Gant, Tyler Parenteau '98*

goat cheese
baby face

The Corridor

Directly west of Eagle's Maw Tower there is a series of tall boulders known as the Corridor, with narrow 1- 2 metre passageways between them.

1. The Bold and the Brave*   5.11b   B (4)   18m
This route starts by clipping your first bolt and then bravely stepping off the ledge with its 3-4 meter drop. Technical, thought-provoking climbing leads up to the crux below the chains. *Geoff Atkins '98*

2. Goat Cheese *   5.11c   B (5)   16m
Just north of the Bold and the Brave, this line is on the extremely green face across from the rather plain-coloured Baby Face. Difficult, sustained climbing on 'holds' which face the wrong way lead you up this stunningly odd looking rock. No walk in the park. Chains. *Paul Gaucher '00*

3. Baby Face   5.9   B (3)   14m
In the narrow corridor directly across from Goat Cheese. This west facing climb offers a mildly featured face which is considerably slabby compared with its counterpart across the passageway. Chains. *Jeff Giebelhaus '00*

Rosstafarian Wall

Across a boulder-strewn gully from Gilligan's Island and on the hike into the Cube is Rosstafarian Wall, an imposing, vertical wall with 1 route on its west face.

4. Gravity Bites ***   5.10d   B (5)   17m
This climb is on the beautifully featured west face, which has a slight depression at the base of the climb. Expect constant interest on cool-looking rock with knee drops and a lot of body movement. Another Field classic, and most likely the best line at the grade. *Mike Ross '98*

Gilligan's Island

Gilligan's Island is a large, boulder-like crag separated from the Cube by a chimney. The best climbs are on the orange east face, with a chasm at the base.

Routes: left to right

5. Little Buddy   5.10c   B (7)   21m
Starts right of a big chimney, with a deep chasm at your back. Weave up a featured slab and put on your thinking cap. Requires good route-finding skills to make it through the crux. Be gentle on the hollow sounding flake just below the chains. *Mike Ross '98*

6. On Shaky Ground   5.10d   B (5)   18m
This is the right-hand line which takes a left-trending path up the featured slab. The name will make sense when you are searching for a way out of the crux and Elvis leg appears. Chains. *Mike Ross '98*

7. SS Minnow   5.11a   15m
An uninspiring face climb on the west side of Gilligan's Island. *Jeff Giebelhaus '98 (no photo)*

"There was no evidence anyone had been there (climbing at the Fields). So we top-roped the chimney (Cool World), then we walked down to look at the Cube. We thought this will never be climbed in a hundred years - its just too steep." Jeff Giebelhaus, 1990, on his discovery trip to the Fields.

The Cube

The Cube is THE centerpiece of the Boulderfields, and can be easily seen from the High Road. All of the routes are too much fun. Exposure: south Routes: left to right.

1. Life of Ryley *   5.10b   B (5)   18m
Far left side. Easy start on tantalizing big holds. Move on to a technical corner feature and finish up by swinging left on to a slab. Chains to lower. *Jeff Giebelhaus '98*

2. Project
Jani has started a new line on the far left of the cube. It is beside the 5.13 project and will share the same start as Life of Riley. *Jani Vaaranpaa '07*

3. Project   5.13-   18m
This awesome line is found 4m right of the Life of Riley. For sure the steepest line at the Fields! Big moves between good holds lead to the obvious wee holds. This route needs a bolt or two; maybe a bolt moved? Some critical hand / foot holds also need reinforcement. *Todd Guy '99*

4. I.M.P. ***   5.12a   B (6)   18m

This is the shit! The best 12a at the Fields! Start below the big flakes and engage the ever-increasing hard cruxes. Heel hooks, high feet and good crimps all the way to the fixed biners to lower. Really good! *Adam Gant, Tyler Parenteau '96*

5. Arachno Dynamic ***   5.12a   B (6)   18m

Another barn burner! Starts in the middle of the Cube to the left of a faint black streak. Climb through on the big holds to an obvious blank section (crux). Finish up with hard moves to the redpoint crux. Do NOT use the small tree below the chains. Again, really good! *Adam Gant, Tyler Parenteau '98*

According to Tyler Parenteau, I.M.P. stands for Impetus For Perfection.

Shauna Jones working Relentless (photo:Steve Jones)

The Cube cont.

6. Trigonometry Lesson**
5.11c   B (6)   18m
Third line in from right corner. More of the same big moves, heel hooks, and a deadpoint crux highlight this pumpy line. Jeff wondered "if it would go" when he bolted this route. Of course it does Jeff, they all do. Chains to lower. *Jeff Giebelhaus '98*

7. Relentless***
5.11b   B (5)   18m
The name says it all. Start 3m from the corner and ride the left-leaning shallow arete. Nice holds and moves which just keep coming lead you all the way to the chains. Good on-sight material if your endurance doesn't fail you on the last few moves. An original hold is gone, making the crux reachy, but it is still an 11b. *Mike Ross '98*

8. Rubix**   5.10c   B (5)   18m
The right hand line which starts at the corner. Is this your warm-up? Or project? Either way, this is one fun journey. Big holds and great clips take you up this steep 10c. Crux at finish with rings for the lower. Bolted on lead. *John Warren, Todd Guy '96*

9. Too Close for Comfort**
5.10b   B (6)   18m
This line is found 'right' around the corner from Rubix. It stands alone on the Cube, simply because it is a slab route. Really fun moves on tight and technical holds with constant interest all the way up. Like we said, completely different than the rest. Chains. *Jeff Giebelhaus '98*

Shit Mix is a bolted (5), scrubbed line set up by James Cruikshank on the west facing slab leading up to the Cube. Intended as an entry route to area, it's probably easier to just do the 'walk-in' approach.

Base 99

A small area which is a 1 minute boulder hop / scramble east of the Cube. Hop or scramble around the chasm on the way to the Cube and to your left (east) is the blocky Base 99. Chains are noticeable, as is the large depression at the start of the routes. Base 99 is southwest facing and host to two 5.11c climbs. Routes: left to right.

1. Base 99**
      5.11c   B (5)   13m
Scramble up a ramp to make the first clip. Now readjust and get your game face on. A nicely sustained line on solid rock and crimpy holds. It lets up right after you clip the big gold chains and yell 'take'. Cool rock, fun. *Tyler Parenteau, Adam Gant '97*

2. Tottering Pine   5.11c   B (4)   13m
Scramble up a loose / chossy ramp to the first bolt. Move up on big positive holds to a thin section (crux). This route falls into the one-move-wonder category. Chains to lower. *Tyler Parenteau, Adam Gant '97*

On the way to the Playground

At the north end of the Centre Field are three small, developed walls known as the Basement, Roadblock and Chalkboard. The Basement is reached via a short left exit off the Centre Field trail near Squall Wall. Roadblock and Chalkboard are directly below the north end ridge trail to the Playground. Farther afield, down the forested gully just past Squall Wall is the Northern Perimeter.

Basement (no photo)

The basement offers 2 top-rope problems, 5.11 and 5.10, set by B. LaBounty in '96.

Roadblock

A black, slabby, scruffy crag about 200 m east of Squall Wall and below the fire-retardant stained north end ridge. Look for the diagonal off-width on the right and a low-lying roof about 2m off the ground on the left. Routes start in the depression at the base of the crag.

Exposure: south   Routes: left to right

1. Impaired
               5.11b   B (5)   15 m
Pull the strenuous roof to the slab above and climb over the overlap at midheight. Quick links to rap. *Tyler Parenteau '01*

2. Smoke Stacks
               5.9   B (7)   20 m
Fight off the raspberry brambles and follow the scruffy diagonal off-width to the fifth bolt. Climb onto the slab and straight up to the top of the crag. Chains. *Tyler Parenteau '01*

Chalkboard

Walk past the Roadblock for about 300m east and you will come to the short, blocky crag called the Chalkboard, so named in reference to its setter's occupation as a teacher.

Exposure: east   Routes: left to right.

3. Praise Beta Allah
               5.9   B(4)   10m
Straightforward climbing to a nice one-move crimp finish. No chains. *Tom Freebairn '97*

4. Exfoliator
               5.10a   B(3)   10m
Weave left to right and vice versa to the chains at the top of the crag. *Tom Freebairn '97*

Northern Perimeter

Walk past Squall Wall and the Playground Trail into the gully. Cairns on your right mark the trail to these two routes. Plans are in the works to expand this area.

Umbellica	5.10c	18m	*Tom Freebairn '98*
Bolters be Damned	5.10d	18m	*Tom Freebairn '98*

Playground

The Playground is a recently developed crag in the northeast corner of the Fields. From Sqaull Wall, it is about a 20 minute hike. From the parking lot, follow the fence line and turn left through gate. Walk along High Road for 5 minutes to the chasm. Hop across or take the small left diversion. The trail angles down Escalator Ramp. Follow the narrow trail to the base of Squall Wall (about 15 minutes from the parking lot). At the far end of Squall, cairns are visible to the right and leading up the hill. Cross the forested gully and head along the top of the red (fire retardant) north ridge. For 20 minutes walk along the scenic trail, then down into the forest and up another slope. Turn slightly left at a cairn-marked boulder, and hop down into the Playground.

The Playground is a unique micro-wonderland consisting of four formations. As you enter, the first one on your right is the Cornerstone, 10 m tall with a distinct razor sharp arete. Farther in and on your left is the east facing 20 m tall Blue Tail, so named because of its resemblance in rock quality to Skaha's Red Tail. Across the way is the crazy-looking Slab Tower, featuring a ramp and a romp. Finally, at the very bottom of the Playground is a south facing, cool formation with a cave in the middle and a ledge at midheight (10m) on the right side.

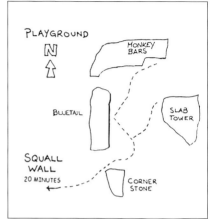

PLAYGROUND

MONKEY BARS

BLUETAIL

SLAB TOWER

SQUALL WALL

20 MINUTES ←

CORNER STONE

Cornerstone

East Face   Routes: left to right

1. Crack Before the Fall   5.9   B (3)   10m
This bolted fist crack starts just right of a tree, and really does not inspire one. There are hangers at the top of the crag. *James Cruikshank*

2. Cornerstone *   5.10a   B (4)   10m
Start as for the crack and clip way out right. Make a thin traverse move up and ride the arete to a nice finish. Pity it's so short. Good rock. Hangers and a quick link to lower. *Jeff Giebelhaus*

North Face

3. Guardian Angel   5.9   B (3)   7m
Scramble up the slope 2m from corner and make a funky move to gain the arete. First move a challenge for short limbs. Hangers only. *Jeff Giebelhaus*

Blue Tail

Exposure: east   Routes: left to right

1. Been Around **   5.10b   B (6)   20m
Start beside a big, detached block. Climb the well-scrubbed route to a very Skaha-type section for the crux. Climbing eases slightly near the top. Good route, really nice rock! Quick links to rap. *Jeff Giebelhaus*

2. Hidden Blumer   5.9   B (4)   20m
Middle line on the crag, which climbs up 2 ledges. Somewhere under all that lichen is a good climb. This route require slightly more 'head space' than its neighbours on either side. Dirty, quick links to rap. *Unknown*

3. Newbie *   5.8   B (5)   20m
Start left of a big crack. Nice climbing on this featured slab, which is thankfully a lot cleaner than its counterpart. Climbing is consistent all the way through. Rings to lower. *Dave MacPherson*

Slab Tower

Exposure: north   Routes: left to right

Two routes; same start in the depression at the bottom of the slab, left to right.

1. The Slab *   5.10a B (9)   24m
Start in the depression and make slippery lichen moves up the slab for 3 bolts. Traverse left under the roof and pull up and over to finish on the low angle slab. Hangers only. *Unknown*

2. Ramp Traverse *   5.9   B (7)   24m
This is the obvious 'up and right' trending ramp which crosses under the Slab Tower. Same start but under the roof swing up and right over a bulge. Follow an awesome finger crack to a station above the end of the ramp. Interesting climb to say the least. Might be fun to try as a mixed route. *James Cruikshank*

Monkey Bars

Monkey Bars lies in the bottom north end of the Playground, behind the base of Slab Tower. Exposure: south Routes: left to right

3. Unknown   5.10a B (3)   10m
Starts just right of the cave in the middle of the crag. Use a combination of jamming the ever-widening crack and crimping the face to reach the ledge at midheight. Quick links to rap. *Unknown*

4. Project   5.12? B (6)   20m
Start just right of a big flake and climb to midheight ledge. Desperate looking finish. Bolting could be an issue! Dangerous climb. Chain and link to lower. *James Cruikshank*
(note: this project is open – any takers?)

Bouldering at the Fields

The potential for exciting, new, futuristic boulder problems at the Fields is vast; all it's going to take is some good old-fashioned work. This inaugural guide is really just to open people's eyes to the area and get the spirit of exploration started. Please keep us posted on blocks you have scrubbed and developed via Mike Shannon at Beyond the Crux Climbing Gym in Kelowna, so we can print it up for the next book. And leave stashed equipment and gear, so problem setters can carry on their good work.

One more thing, pretty much all of the bouldering photos were done by April Smith, co-owner of Beyond the Crux, so we are just gonna say they are all hers. Thanks so much, April!

above: Mike Shannon on Bigglesworth, with Chris de Vries spotting.

Bigglesworth

Shark

*above left: Chris de Vries cranking on Bigglesworth   bottom right: Mike Doyle on Shark Boulder
facing: Easy to see how Shark Boulder got its name.*

64

Ridge Trail

Bigglesworth Boulder

One minute past the gate and down the Ridge Trail on your left.

1. (V4) Fat Shannon's Drop
Low start under the overhang. Crux to some small holds on the lip.
Follow crimps to an easy top out. *Mike Shannon*

Shark Boulder

Near Wonderbar. Exposure: north   Routes: left to right.

1. (V6) Meat Works
Left side of the Shark's Nose, feet planted on the steep face. Up and
right to a slopy top out. *Chris de Vries*

2. (V10) Fraser Island
Right side of Shark's Nose, up and over the 'nose' for a slopy top
out. Close but not yet.

Meat Locker

Chime Zilla

Chime Zilla

1 2 3 4 5

above: Nate Woods on Sharp Salad, Chime Zilla

Meat Locker

Meat Locker is a chasm of sorts found southeast
from Shark Boulder. Have multiple pads and spotters as there is a slab at your back.

Left of Chimney
Two problems which ascend a featured face. Both are V1 with sit starts. They go at V4
and V3 respectively. *Nate Woods, Mike Doyle*

Right of Chimney   Routes: left to right

1. (V3) Rasta Crack
Start just right of arete and trend up and right to the spooky mantle. *Mike Shannon*

2. (V6) All The Way With Stephanie Kay
Sit start down and right from last problem. Boulder up and left on rounded and pointy
holds to the same spooky mantle. *Chris de Vries*

Chime Zilla

Chime Zilla is located 30 meters south of Wonderbar Wall on the approach to the
Bismark. Similar to The Meat Locker (chasm), but these problems are on 2 faces that
oppose each other. The north face is steeper with 2 problems, while the south face is
steep but instead of top-outs, you traverse left to exit problems.

South Face   Routes: left to right

1. (V0) Sharp Salad
Low start on some awkward holds to a deadpoint for a good hold at the lip. Exit left.
Mike Shannon

2. (V0) Dice
Low start, the obvious line of weakness on big positive holds in the middle of the face.
Exit left. *Mike Shannon*

3. (V1) Dice Direct
Low start on right side of face. A bit more challenging than Sharp Salad. Boulder up
and left, again exit left. *Mike Shannon*

North Face   Routes: left to right

4. (V6) Copyright Infringement
Left side of short steep face. Low start, small holds and crimps to an all out deadpoint
at the lip. *Chris de Vries*

5. (V1)) Piece of Shit Rail
Right side of face, sit start direct. The name says it all. Ride some positive features up
and slightly right to the mantle. *Chris de Vries*

Cairn

Cairn Boulder

Cairn is below Little Pika, on the Southeast Trail, and near F1 Boulder.

1. (V2) Slopy Poo-Poo. Sit start on the north-east aspect of short boulder. You can't get this one wrong. *Chris de Vries*

facing page:
Brian Gibbons on
Shoemaker Shuffle

F1 east face

Southeast Trail

The Southeast Trail is host to most of the developed bouldering problems - lots of future potential too! Upcoming stellars near Stepping Stone.

F1 Boulder

East Face   Routes: left to right

1. (V2) Push It To The Max
Same sit start as last, but move up and left on much more demanding holds to a more awkward mantle. *Mike Shannon*

2. (V1) Bravo
Sit start just left of the opening and pull straight up to the same mantle as last problem. *Mike Shannon*

3. (V0) Sausage Pickle 2000.com
Sit start far right and traverse the obvious rail system left to the weakest point. *Mike Shannon*

North Face   Routes: left to right (steep)

4. (V5) Shoemaker Shuffle
Sit start on the left side with a small boulder at your back. A deadpoint to a good hold gets you set up to move right on crimps and slopers. Mantle the 'peak' right in the middle. *Chris de Vries*

5. (V9) Nelly's Thin Thins
Sit start in the middle and make use of the crimps. The next 3 moves are real thin. Shares the same mantle as last. *Chris de Vries*

6. (V7) V Power
Sit start on the right side with hands matched on a slightly detached flake. A hard pull to a downward sloping rail sets you up to finish slightly left. *Chris de Vries*

east

north

west

1a 1

2

3 4

5

5 6 7

above and facing page: Lucy Rodina on Surf Boulder (east and west faces)

Nerf Boulder - Located 1 minute directly north of the Surf Boulder. A great piece of rock and a really fun area to play at. There are a few proud highballs, but as of press time they have not been bouldered yet.

Surf Boulder

Found just below Pterodactyl / Northern Exposure Crags. A good mix of problems from the west facing highballs to the north face (steep), and an obvious lowball traverse on the east side.

1. (V5) Kelowna Fornication
Sit start 2m left of the corner on two very obvious holds. Boulder up and right, traversing towards the corner. Mantle out just around the corner at the obvious weakness. *Chris de Vries* (1a. V1 variation. Forget the traverse - pull up and over.)

2. (V7) Don't You Know Who You Think I Am
Sit start slightly on the left of the corner and make 3 long hard moves straight up to mantle (crimpy features). *Lyle Saunders*

3. (V3) Meat Pickle
Sit start slightly right and make a big move up and right to a good hold. Finish with a few moves on some lovely crimps straight up. Easy mantle. *Cody Laden*

4. (V7) Axle Rose
Same sit start as Meat Pickle, but trend up and right on slopy crimps. Huge finishing move off a left hand crimp to a distant hold on the lip. Awesome line. *Chris de Vries*

5. (V5) Slashed Snake Bite
A smooth, rounded arete with an obvious slot for a few fingers. Start just right of the arete and move around the corner to the steep face, then up on crimps just left of detached feature. *Chris de Vries*

6. (V1) Round One
A crimpy, vertical highball which moves towards the big hold up high and the obvious 'exit' notch. *Rob Bannatyne*

7. (V1) The Chipper
Far right side of face, climb the arete using face holds and the arete towards the big point. Exit on top of boulder. *Jani Vaaranpaa*

7

Ladybug

right: Jani working Cave Dweller
above facing: Chris De Vries on Ladybug

Ladybug Boulder

Ladybug Boulder is 1 minute east of Surf Boulder and just before Oriental Garden, on the Southeast Trail to the Dark Side.

1. (V2) Ladybug Strikes Back
Sit start with hands matched on the obvious rail, boulder up and left for the crux mantle. *Jani Vaaranpaa*

2. (V1) Lola Ladybug
Same sit start as last, but boulder up and right to the weakest point for an easy mantle. *Jani Vaaranpaa*

3. (V3) Lazy Ladybug
Start at the far right, and make some gnarly open handed moves, traversing left until you can mantle out at the end of Lola Ladybug. *Jani Vaaranpaa*

Cave Dweller Boulder

1. (V2) Warmup
Left side of cave, four moves to the mantle, useful warm-up for the cave. *Rob Bannatyne*

2. (V4/5) Cave Dweller
The obvious steep line which starts in the depression. A few welcoming moves lead to the all out deadpoint for the lip. Sit start anyone? *Chris de Vries*

White Spot

3. (V2) Baby Slab
A 4m high slab problem with small crimps and side pulls to a final reach for the top.

3a.(V0) variation - same problem, but use the arete on your right to bring the grade down. *Jani Vaaranpaa*

4. (V3) My Latest Mistake
Directly around the right corner from Baby Slab. A stellar line which starts with a match off a good rail down low and follows positive crimps to the top-out. Really good. *Jani Vaaranpaa*

3   3a   4

Cedar Mountain Regional Park was so named in part because of an abundance of tall, proud cedar trees in this region. The 1993 Okanagan Mountain Park Class 6 (worst category) firestorm changed all of that. (A firestorm is when the heat is so intense it creates its own wind. Firestorms also happen after nuclear bombings.)

On August 16, after months of virtually no rain, the historic fire started with a lightning strike. For a month the sun blazed red through ash whiteouts, and the air quality index often climbed past 200 (anything above 40 is considered poor air quality). At night, the sky turned red, the fire looked like lava on the black mountain ridges, and trees exploded from the heat. The fire consumed over 250 square km (the city of Kelowna is approx. 262 square km), 239 homes, and forced the evacuation of 27,000 people, the largest evacuation in the shortest period of time in Canadian history.

Cedar Park .... *map* 76

It is amazing to watch the rebirth of this region. Flowers and birds are plentiful, views are spectacular, and the climbing just keeps getting better.

above: Cedar Park climbing area. (Aerial shot : Mike Shannon, Pilot: Tyler McNabb)

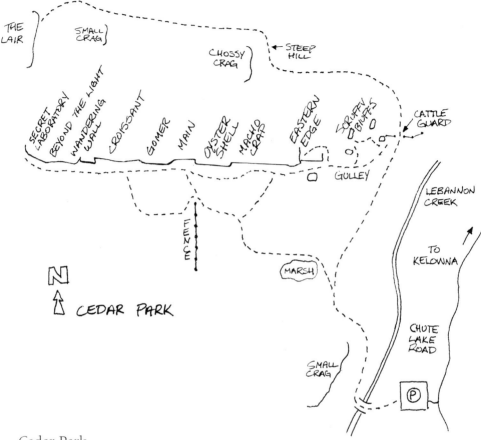

THE LAIR

SMALL CRAG

CHOSSY CRAG

STEEP HILL

SECRET LABORATORY

BEYOND THE LIGHT

WANDERING WALL

CROISSANT

GOMER

MAHN

OYSTER SHELL

MACHO CRAFT

EASTERN EDGE

SCRUFFY BLUFFS

CATTLE GUARD

GULLEY

LEBANNON CREEK

TO KELOWNA

FENCE

N

CEDAR PARK

MARSH

CHUTE LAKE ROAD

SMALL CRAG

P

Cedar Park

Also referred to as the Kelowna Crags or the
Main Crags, Cedar Park was first used as a trad playground for Leon Blumer, Eric Rayson and
the rest of the mountaineering boys of the '60s. With the exception of Moonlight Sonata ('60s),
Buckle Up ('60s) and Ticked Off ('90s), all of the classic trad routes – Chain Lightning,
Spiderman, Noisy Oyster, Trick or Treat – were developed in the '80s.

It was the 1990's, however, that became the most prolific era for route development at Cedar
Park. Back then, sport climbing was the new craze, but there was a catch. If you wanted to sport
climb, you needed a rope, harness, shoes - and a drill. Todd Guy, Adam Gant, Tyler Parenteau,
Mike Ross and Jeff Giebelhaus were the big-time bolters of the day.

Today Cedar Park has over 100 sport routes on the main crag, the Scruffy Bluffs and the Lair.
There is a terrific variety of bolted routes, particularly in the 10s and 11s, most of the stations are
in good repair, and all can be done with a 60m rope.

There are about 20 trad routes at Cedar Park, most in the 5.6 –5.9 range, with a few burly 10s. A 70m rope will get you safely on everything, but you can make-do with a 60m and a knot (we did). The classics are truly must-dos, and generally in good repair. The other routes need some traffic to get them back to their prime. In general, the trad lines offer two pitch options, a bit of fancy footwork and the occasional heroic gear placement. For alpine enthusiasts, give these fun routes some love, and, if you clip a brush to your rack, a bit of maintenance too!

The main wall of Cedar Park is south facing, so mornings and evenings are ideal in the hot summer. The Lair is east facing in a wide valley, so offers up more shade options.

above: Diane Doyle, Expressway, pitch one, (photo: Barbara Crawford)

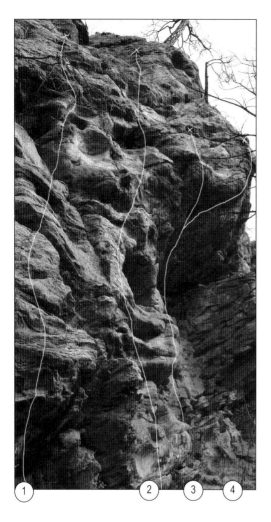

Secret Laboratory

Secret Laboratory is located at the far west end of Cedar Park, which is about 5 minutes from Croissant Wall. The bluff is easy to identify with its showcase steep wall, large hueco holds and a fun ramp leading up to the steep section.

Exposure: south   Routes: left to right.

1. Bulldogs *
                5.10b   B(4)   14m
Far left line on the wall. A featured buttress which ends with a distinct bulge at the top. Chains. *Marty Zikmund '97*

2. The Last Line *
                5.8   B(4)   14m
The line of bolts which starts just left of the steep hueco face and offers up straightforward, low angle climbing on big holds and pockets. Lots and lots of features on this one. *Jeff Giebelhaus '97*

3. Guinea Pig *
                5.11b   B(3)   12m
Scramble up an easy ramp towards a really big hueco pocket, and make your first clip. A few tweaky moves and gaston lead you to a flat-topped ledge. A distant hold below the station seems to be your only option. *Adam Gant, Tyler Parenteau '97*

4. The Scenic Route **
                5.11c   B(4)   14m
Same start as Guinea Pig, but after the first clip, boulder out right on the lip of the roof. Reach the seam and it is time for a big move and the finishing romp on crimps. Sustained and fun, the gym crowd will like this journey. *Adam Gant, Tyler Parenteau '97*

The first book on Kelowna climbing was Andrew Sauter's Kelowna Crags - An Informal Guide to Rock Climbing in the Central OK (early '90s). In 1996, Lyle Knight authored Central BC Rock, which featured Kelowna rock climbs. Three years later, Dean Urness and the Alpine Club of Canada published Rockclimbs - Kelowna and Area (1999).

Beyond the Light

Another short crag located 30m east of Secret Laboratory. This crag features a small overhang on the left, a slight bulge in the middle, and a left-facing corner at the far right.

Exposure: south   Routes: left to right.

1. Pull Into The Light *   5.10b   B(5)   14 m
This is the most traveled line on this crag. Climb up a slabby ramp to a steep section of wall, clip a bolt and crux through to a more obvious line of climbing on solid, featured rock. Chains. *Adam Gant, Tyler Parenteau '97*

2. Immortal Balance *   5.10b   B(5)   14 m
Starts 2m to the right of Pull Into the Light. Climb to a ledge at the base of a distinct bulge and figure out a safe way to go and get the first bolt clipped. Follow the smooth bulge to the same station as last climb. *Adam Gant, Tyler Parenteau '97*

3. Weak Puppy
       5.9   B(3)   15 m
Located just 2m left of the corner. A face climb which ascends a smooth, but featured wall. Chains. *Adam Gant, Tyler Parenteau '97*

4. 2-Nuts
       5.7   Trad   10 m
The west facing crack, between the corner and the arete. As the name implies, that is probably the extent of the rack you need to lead this one. Ends at a small ledge and there are some crusty chains to lower. *Marty Zikmund '97*

Cedar Park and the Lonely Crags are accessible for dogs. As with any public place, consider your dog's social skills before heading in, and make sure to bring lots of water for your four-legged friend, as shade is minimal. That's Nelson in the photo.

Wandering Wall

There are 7 trad and bolted lines in this area, which extends from Beyond the Light to Croissant Wall. It begins with a 3-bolt-wonder on a very short buttress, to the imposing, right-facing dihedral 20m left of Excessive Speed.

Exposure: south
Routes: left to right

1. Stranger In a Strange Land
    5.7   B(3)   8 m
A short face climb which ascends a featured, low-angled face. Easy to locate with the fist crack feature to its right and a left corner feature just off the face. Could be a nice first lead. *Scott Jeffries, early '90s*

The next two climbs start below 2 distinct corners and end at the ledge with a burnt-out tree for a station.

2. Wizard
    5.6   Trad   16 m
This is the left-hand corner feature. Start with an easy scramble up to a ledge 5m off the deck. Follow the low-angled corner to tree and station. *Farley Klotz, Andrew Sauter, early '90s.*

3. Lichen Corner
    5.4   Trad   16 m
Same start as the last climb. Once you gain the lower ledge, take on the lower crescent-shaped corner feature. As the name implies, this one has not seen a wire brush. Same station as Wizard. Eric *Rayson, Leon Blumer, late '60s*

The landmark tree at Croissant Wall. Two years ago a windstorm pummeled us with its bark. Now it is quite bare and beautiful.

⑥ ⑦

The next four climbs are all grouped together around the two long (50+m) corner/dihedral systems.

4. Cadillac Ranch
        5.7   Trad 2 pitches   50 m
Stand at the base of Cyclops Eye. To your left there is a fixed sling hanging at the 20m mark, near a blocky outcrop. Climb to this point and belay your second up. Weave up the loose-featured face to the top of the crag and set a natural station to finish. Loose rock. Good route-finding skills required. The rack: CDs to 2.5" / nuts / long slings. *Eric Rayson, '60s*

5. Cyclops Eye
        5.6 RX   2 pitches 55 m
The obvious, intimidating chimney. A long run-out makes falling out of the question. At 30m you will reach the 'eye' opening in the chimney. Set a station here to belay your second up. Nice climbing leads to the top of the crag and a good natural station. Loose rock and natural hazards. The rack: long slings / small and medium CDs / a few larger nuts. *Eric Rayson, Leon Blumer, late '60s*

6. Breakaway   5.11c   B(9)   45 m
The belay bolt for this route is ironically placed on the neighbouring trad line, Cheops. Climb the headwall in a convoluted, weaving path. Watch for loose blocks. The poorly located station wreaks havoc on your rope as you lower. *Dean Urness, Dave Urness '97*

7. Cheops   5.6 R   Trad   55 m
The right-facing dihedral just left of Croissant Wall. This can be done in 1 pitch using lots of long runners to avoid drag. The 2 cruxes are well-protected with large cams, and the route has a good natural station at the top of the crag. Loose rock and natural hazards. The rack: CDs to 4" / a big hex / long slings. *Bud Godderies, late '60s*

Jani and I were trying to figure out what kind of gear to use for the gaping chimney of Cyclops Eye. Eric Rayson answered our question on lead - none! Above: Eric is just entering the Eye. Photo John Lang

Croissant Wall

Named for its shape and flakiness, Croissant Wall is a must-do if in your firing range. Jani and John Lang set up 6 routes in the 2 years following the Okanagan Mountain Park Fire - hence the name, Up From the Ashes (almost named Phoenix Rising). Exposure: south   Routes: left to right.

1 Excessive Speed *   5.11c   B(4)   12 m
The far left route on Croissant Wall, located 20m to the right of the big dihedral. Pull up on a big jug ledge to get established and climb through to a rest under the short roof. A crux clip and bouldery sequence guard the rusty hook station. *Todd Guy '95*

2. Trads Gone Mad *   5.11b   B(6)   15 m
Three metres right of Excessive Speed. Look for the left-trending ramp just above the first clip. After the fourth bolt crux moves grab jugs all the way to the poorly rigged, fixed station. Seems easier than its neighbor to the left. *John Warren, Ken Woodward '95*

3. See The Light **   5.11c   B(8)   20 m
Same start as last line, but head right toward the fixed chain, then under an overlap for a welcome rest. A series of cruxes involving high feet and deadpoints highlight this super-fun line. *Todd Guy '96*

4. Strange Currency ***   5.11d   B(9)   22 m
Engaging climbing on reinforced (glued) flakes lead to a jug at the
top of a left-trending feature. Shake it out, and cross a cruxy wall
to a ledge. Crimps, jugs, and high feet carry you through this
pumpy line to a station with fixed 'biners. *Todd Guy'95*

5. Up From The Ashes **   5.11b   B(9)   22 m
John's first classic foray up Croissant Wall after the firestorm. A
reachy move to a huge jug leads to a right-facing feature and a
wild finish on jugs. A spoiler crux before reaching the station,
shared by Strange Currency. *John Lang, Bearheart Desrosieres '05*

6. Mohawks On Belay **   5.11b   B(9)   22 m
Same start as Ashes, but take the right line of bolts. Head up high
towards the white wall with a black streak. Reachy moves followed
by awesome bucket-tugging over very steep rock. It leaves you
with a smile. Huge hooks to lower. *John Lang, Jani Vaaranpaa '06*

7. Desperation **   5.11d   B(8)   25 m
The good climbs on Croissant Wall continue! Scramble up on big
ledges, deal with a blank vertical wall, then romp through to a
no-hands rest under the big imposing roof. Compose yourself,
then thank the Creator for time spent in the gym as you pull this
roof. Another rusty hook station. *Mike Doyle '97*

8. 51 Hot Dogs **   5.11a   B(10)   25 m
Three metres right of Desperation. The low first bolt protects a
high step to a good ledge. Long reaches and big holds make up
most of the climb. The real fun is the very airy and exposed left
step across a blank-faced bulge with a bolt on it. A steep jughaul
up and over finishes the gig. A popular route. *John Lang '06*

9. Razor's Edge *   5.11c   B(10)   25 m
Same start as 51 Hot Dogs, but move right after the fifth bolt. Long
reaches on open-handed holds take you to yet another steep,
pumpy finish. *John Lang '06*

10. Hang Time *   5.11d   B(9)   25 m
Starts about 20m right of 51 Hot Dogs. Climb towards a big ledge
via a tantalizing, detached flake. A short wall takes you under the
left-trending roof. From here a boulder problem guards the chain
station. It's a shame there's so much 5.10 climbing for a 5.11 roof
problem. *Jani Vaaranpaa, Jason Crumb '06*

Ludo Bourdon,
Mohawks on Belay

11. Then There Was Three *
    5.10c   B(6)   23 m
This ugly climb starts 3m right of Hang Time, and heads for a big ledge. It helps to be tall on the reachy crux, then it's just plain fun as you pull on those big huecos up the steep wall. *Jani Vaaranpaa, John Lang '05*

12. Rocky Mountain Fever **
    5.10a   B(6)   22 m
It's always good entertainment watching people deal with the grovel mantle at the fourth clip. Happy, exposed climbing to an in-your-face crux. The chains are hidden in an alcove. The solid stone is probably better than Yam! *Jeff Giebelhaus '97*

13. Never Too Late
    5.7   B(3)   12 m
Far right line on Croissant Wall. Face climbing on a nicely featured slab leads to question mark finish. Scramble over big blocks to a station with quick links on a smooth wall. This is Lee's first go as a route setter. *Lee Sheppard, Diane Doyle '07*

Kevin McLane and Howie Richardson (former and current authors of Skaha Rockclimbs) grew up in the same area of Newcastle Upon Tyne, England, but never met until they had both emigrated to Canada.

Above: Kevin McLane climbing Rocky Mountain Fever, as part of his research on the Kelowna section of his most recent guidebook - Canadian Rock: Select Rockclimbs of the West.

Gomer Wall

Gomer Wall is a popular climbing spot with its assortment of moderate climbs on solid stone. It is host to Expressway, which extends to the top of crag and is currently the only 3-pitch route in Kelowna. According to Eric Rayson, Gomer Wall was originally known as Rannoch Wall, one of his favourite places to climb in Scotland.

Gomer Wall is beside Croissant Wall and 2 minutes west (left) of the landmark climb, Chain Lightning, on Main Wall. Gomer features a distinct belay ledge, with 2 high belay bolts for the first 4 climbs. If you are looking for fun sub-5.10 climbing, then this is the wall for you. Keep in mind its great exposure and ledgey face can be a little intimidating to new leaders.

Exposure: south   Routes: left to right.

1. Birthday Present   5.10a   B(7)   25 m
Swing out left and straight up. *Jeff Giebelhaus '97*

2. Squeeze Me In   5.9   B(9)   26 m
The newest addition to Gomer Wall. The name says it all; it's a squeeze play which ascends the wall just left of the small roof. Loose rock. New leaders will find comfort in having plenty of bolts. Evelyn Ens gives it a thumbs up. *Lee Sheppard, Diane Doyle '07*

above: Evelyn Ens on the second pitch of Expressway.

85

3. Southern Comfort *   5.10b   B(6)   24 m
The most technically demanding line on Gomer Wall. Lovely, delicate face-climbing
leads to the small cruxy roof up high. Once you have the beta, the roof goes easier than
it looks at first glance. Hanna's favourite Gomer climb. *Jeff Giebelhaus '97*

4. Give Me Face *   5.7   B(5)   24 m
The line left of the red hangers, directly below a belay bolt. This route offers great
stone and pause for reflection as you look above and the bolts get spaced farther apart.
Chains. *Jeff Giebelhaus, Kerry McAbe '97*

5. Gomer Line **   5.9   B(6)   25m
The original Gomer line. A very popular, classic route, easily identified by the red
hangers. The route meanders close to the bolt line, with a couple of well-protected
crux moves near the top. Chains. *Scott Jeffries '95*

facing page: Jake Orr (left) and Jason Duris (right) setting stations on Gomer Wall.

6. The Generator *   5.8   B(7)   25 m

This is the face climb right of the red hangers. The opening move over the roof is the crux. Once again, solid stone and interesting climbing leads to a chain station. Slings are a good idea when setting a top-rope station; otherwise the rope drag is huge. *Marty Zikmund, Jeff Giebelhaus '97*

(Note: there is a second pitch for Generator that goes at 5.10a and ends up in the right-facing dihedral up top. It looks beautiful, but there is nothing pretty about the loose rock and odd bolt placement. Not recommended!)

7. Expressway ***   (P1) 5.9   (P2) 5.8   (P3) 5.7   B(8)   78m

A great multi-pitch line, with the first pitch being the toughest and best quality. Start on the Gomer ledge. Traverse around the corner and over to the slab wall for the next 2 pitches. Finish off with a lovely 5.8 roof. There is also a 5.10c left variation on the final pitch bolted by Jeff Giebelhaus. You have the option of walking off, or rapping (use a 60m rope with a knot). *Mike Ross '96*

Yellow Wall

The next four climbs start 10m up the hill and right of Expressway. Yellow Wall is easy to identify by its colour and the left-facing crack with its wonderful off-width (Spiderman).

Exposure: south
Routes: left to right

1. Put Off by Lichen **
5.11a   Mixed(2)   20 m
Left of Spiderman. This is an excellent line, with bomber cam placements and delicate face moves leading up to 2 bolts placed below the bulge. The exit moves over the bulge are really quite exciting. Bring CDs up to 1.5 ". Rap station is on the ledge. *John Warren, Ken Woodward '94*

2. Spiderman **   5.10   Trad   20 m
This is the obvious off-width roof with a left-facing crack ending at the same ledge/station as the last climb. Bring a #4 Camalot to protect the burly crux of getting up and around the roof. There is a very rusty piton 2/3 of the way up, but some medium CDs and nuts should see you through to the station. *Unknown '80s*

3. Tiny Testicles *   5.10-   Trad   30 m
Same start as Spiderman, but just before the roof swing out and right. Head up on good holds to a devious hard-to-read crux (nicely protected). Follow the faint seam and end on a big ledge with a chain station shared by Moonlight Sonata. Tie your end knot, as it is a full 30m rappel! The rack: small nuts / CDs to 1.5" *Rick Cox '80s*

4. Moonlight Sonata ***   5.7   Trad   30 m
A '60s Trad classic. Follow left-trending ramp up to a tree. Use the hand crack on the right or follow the finger crack on the left. Keep moving left on easy ground to a large ledge with a shared station (Tiny Testicles). Another full 30 m rappel. The rack: nuts and CDs to 2". *Leon Blumer, Eric Rayson '60s (photo page 91, route marked MS.)*

Moonlight Sonata on the Yellow Wall is one of Leon Blumer's favourite climbs, and so named because the boys were 'nighted' by the time they finished setting the route. In 1952 Leon climbed 26 European peaks, and in 1958 he was part of the party that made the first ascent of Alaska's Mount Blackburn (west face). Leon gave us a hand with research for Kelowna Rock. Above he compares notes with Hanna, as daughter Louise looks on. Photo by John Lang.

Main Wall

Main Wall consists of a left and right section, neatly broken in half by the amazing trad line Chain Lightning (distinctly lightning-like in appearance). Main Wall offers up a nice mix of technical 5.10 - 11 sport climbs, and finishes at the classic trad line, Noisy Oyster.

Exposure: south   Routes: left to right

1. Dr. Dave *   5.10c   B(8)   22 m
Far left line of bolts, 2m right of Moonlight Crack. Climb up on the boulder to begin. Tight technical climbing leads to a right-facing corner dish feature. Metolious hangers to lower. *Dean Urness, Mike Scott '96*

2. Not A Toy *   5.10d   B(6)   18 m
The second line of bolts just right of the raised boulder platform. Again, tight technical climbing leads to a very hard-to-read crux and then on to a chain station. *Todd Guy, Rob Monteith '96*

3. Rat's Tooth *   5.11a   B(6)   18 m
A Kelowna classic as far as slabs go. This technical line trends up and left, ending near the Chain Lightning roof. Crux is very much 'on your feet' as you head towards the third bolt. Bolted station. *Kirby Dunstan '85*

4. The Lazy Bumble Bee *   5.11c   B(10)   28 m
Starts 3m left of Chain Lightning. Follow 3 bolts towards the imposing roof. Pull the roof (crux) then continue on scruffy 5.10- climbing to the chain station. *Dean Urness, Betty Urness '97*

5. Pistachio *   5.10c   B(4)   18 m
Same start as Chain Lightning. Run it out unprotected to the obvious undercling, then reach over the overlap and clip a bolt. This climb features a series of balance-critical cruxes all the way to the beefy chains. *Tyler Parenteau, Tyler Mack '02*

6. Chain Lightning ***   5.9   Trad   30 m
A stunning gear line which trends up and left under a roof to the left-facing feature. Bomber gear and solid rock highlight this Kelowna classic. The rack: nuts / CDs to 2". Note that it is exactly a 30 m rappel (tie a knot) from chain station! *Vic Kramer '80s*

7. Black Lung ***   5.10c   B(11)   30 m
A great journey which starts 3m right of Chain Lightning crack. A left-trending seam leads you to a stiff crux. Finish up with an airy finish through a steep notch in the crag. Chains. *Jeff Giebelhaus '96*

More Eric Rayson trivia: In almost 5 decades of climbing, the only bail gear EVER left by the renowned international mountaineer was on his failed on-sight attempt of Noisy Oyster in the 1970s. It was not until 1984 that brothers Chris and Kirby Dunstan finally sent this amazing route. Eric continues to enjoy climbing.

left: Dean Urness on Kelowna One, one of his favourite Cedar Park routes. (Photo courtesy Dean)

Main Wall cont.

8. Detour **   5.10b   B(10)   25 m
Another nicely bolted line, up a left-trending ramp. Deal with the route-finding crux,
and exit through an open book at the roof above. There are 2 runout bolts above the
chimney, where the climbing eases up. Nice exposure. Chains. *Jeff Giebelhaus late '90s*

9. Point of Impact   5.10c   B(11)   30 m
As the name suggests, this climb has claimed some victims. Start 2m right of last
climb, just left of an upward left-trending ramp. After a challenging start, follow the
bolts on sloper holds up the solid face and over the roof at the 20m mark. A nice, airy
finish high on the face. Chains. *Mike Ross '96*

10. A Kind End ***   5.10a   B(11)   30 m
Yet another lovely, steep, sustained bolted line. Climb a detached flake to the first bolt
and cast off on solid rock, cruxing over the bulges. Head up towards the roof and
finish high on the solid headwall. Nicely bolted. Chains. *Jeff Giebelhaus, John Lang '02*

11. Take Your Time   5.10c   B(7)   22 m
Start 3m left of the obvious corner/crack (Noisy Oyster). Three bolts lead you up a
left-trending seam to easier climbing. For some unobvious reason there are 2 closely
spaced bolts near the top. Chain station. *Dean Urness '98*

12. Noisy Oyster ***   5.10-   Trad 2P   38m
Start in the burly-looking corner crack. Solid jams and face holds lead you out and
left, and then up a right-facing crack to a chain station at 20m. *Dunstan Brothers '84*

13 The second pitch for Noisy Oyster is 18m and not as interesting as pitch one. Cast
up and right towards a right-facing book and finish at the sling. The second station is
at approximately 38m. The rack: Nuts / CDs up to 2.5". *Chris Dunstan, Kirby Dunstan '84*

Oyster Shell

Exposure: south Routes: left to right

1. Reaching for Shania's Slot *   5.11b   B(4)   12 m
The short, powerful, steep bulge 2m right of Noisy Oyster. Good jugs and crimps lead
up the steep face to a blank headwall for the crux up top. A little scruffy and dirty at
the crux. *Todd Guy, late '90s*

2. Trick or Treat **   5.8   Trad   35 m
Start 5m right of Shania's Slot. Climb a left-trending crack with bomber gear and jams,
to a low angled corner/crack system. Mid-station finish at 24m consists of a rusted
rivet and new hanger, or continue up more crack/corner features to a chain station up
and right. Good pro. The rack: nuts / CDs up to 2.5". *Rick Cox, Chris Dunstan '80s*

Oyster Shell cont.

The following 3 climbs are reached by scrambling up and right from the base of 'Trick or Treat'. There is a comfortable ledge 8m off the ground with a belay bolt.

3. Don't Date Teddy Bears (aka DDT) *   5.11b   B(4)   25 m
From the belay bolt, trend up and left toward a dead tree and wild-looking roof. Pull the roof (fun), then follow up with a thin move to a bulge. A bolt seems to be missing after the bulge, but a small cam can protect the final run-out to the chains (Blue Metolius). *Dean Urness, Chris Leachman '96*

4. Not So Soft **   5.11b   M(4)   25 m
Head straight up the slab from the belay bolt to a left-facing corner feature and roof. A cruxy roof leads to a welcome rest before the steep, juggy finish. A nice mixed line which requires nuts and CDs to 1.5". Chain station. *Dean Urness, Chris Leachman '96*

5. Grin and Grunt It   5.11c   B(6)   25 m
Climb the line of bolts which trends up and right from belay bolt. Three clips lead to a blank-looking bulge. A hard-to-read sequence gets you up and over to a good stance. The next bolt is still way above, so you may want small nuts to protect a thin move before the last clip. An odd station awaits for the lower-off. *Dean Urness, J.C.Lapierre '02*

The next two climbs start at an obvious ledge (with a belay bolt) left of Bull N Bush corner.

6. Kelowna One   5.10+   Mixed   32 m
Originally a trad route, but bolts on other climbs now interfere with this left trending line. From the belay bolt, climb up the left-facing corner to a handrail traverse. Continue up to another left-facing corner feature and under a small roof. Step left and around small roof to finish at DDT station. Rack: nuts, cams up to 2". *Kirby Dunstan, Chris Dunstan '85*

7. French Connection   5.10b   B(6)   25 m
Gingerly move up and right over suspect rock and a very loose, big flake. Pull the crux bulge and scramble up a slab towards the right-facing corner with a bolt. Big jugs to an exposed move left of the last bolt. Chains. *Dean Urness, J.C.Lapierre '02*

8. Bull N Bush   P1 5.7   Trad   30 m
Pitch 1 is the obvious right-facing corner that finishes with a big chimney (big stretch for small legs) exit to a grassy ledge. This is best described as an adventure climb as you will have to bushwhack your way up the corner at times. There is also loose rock and debris along the climb. *Leon Blumer, Eric Rayson '60s*

9. Pitch 2   Dolly Parton Overhand   P2 5.6   Trad   30 m
Build your station using the bomber horizontal slot at chest height, about 4 m left of chimney exit (save two 1" CDs). Climb up 18m, to the left side of the long roof and continue up scruffy rock. Once on top of the crag, there is a large fallen tree about 10m from the edge to anchor the belay station. The rack: nuts, CDs to 3.5". *Rick Cox, Don Skuratoff '83*

Macho Crap Wall

This area is for trad climbers, and is located right of the plethora of overhead ropes (press time). Mountaineer Dave Jones spent two years working on a multi-pitch routes to the top, between Oyster Shell and Macho Crap. As of print time the routes are not finished. Do not climb on these ropes.

Exposure: south   Routes: left to right

1. Formicator   5.7   Trad   30 m
An unappealing trad line 4m right of Bull N Bush. The line ends at a ledge with no station. *Ron Collins, Barry Jones '92*

2. Ticked Off**   5.8   Trad   25 m
This is the beautiful right-facing crack feature 14m from the Bull N Bush corner. Really fun climbing with bomber gear placements and great stances, followed by an airy crux halfway up. Chain station. Rack: Nuts, CDs to 1.5". *Ron Collins, Peter Mair '92*

3. Out There   5.9R   Trad   25 m
This is a dangerous, runout route. Same start as Ticked Off, but step out and right 2m to access a right-facing crack feature which leads to a short roof. The rock is dirty and suspect when facing crux right of the roof. Same station as last climb. *Andrew Sauter, Ron Collins '93*

4. Solstice   5.9R   Trad   25 m
Starts 3m left of the bolted Macho Crap. A weaving line with run-out pro. Probably best avoided. Use Macho Crap station. *Ron Collins, Roger Pickering '92*

5. Macho Crap*   5.10b   B (6)   25 m
The nicely spaced line of bolts that travels through a series of bulges and slabs to a chain belay, located on a narrow ledge.

6. Pitch 2   P2   Mixed   30 m
The second pitch heads up to a roof with a bolt. There is a tree with a sling for a station. Walk off right. *Gary MacCallum, John Warren '94*

7. Bowling Ball**   5.8   Trad   25 m
The left-facing crack/corner feature. Interesting, fun climbing with bomber pro lead you up this menacing-looking line. Macho Crap station. Nuts and CDs to 2". *Leon Blumer, Eric Rayson '60s*

8. Project   B (3)   8 m
A line of studs up a steep roof with very hard-looking moves. This is 20m right of Bowling Ball, and an open project. Any setters interested? *Todd Guy*

left: Macho Crap Wall. Circles indicate climbers, and if you look closely at the top of Dolly Parton Overhand (writeup page .95) you will see the tree we used as an anchor for the station.

Eastern Edge

Eastern Edge begins around the corner of the main crag on the east facing white wall that runs along Toboggan Ledge. Scramble up and right from the overhang.

Toboggan Ledge

1. Buy Your Ticket **

   5.10c   B(5)   15 m

Far left line with red hangers above the second clip. Fun, friendly climbing on big sloper holds leads past a horizontal break and then up and over a ledge into an alcove. Quick links to rap. *Todd Guy '94*

2. Gamelan

   5.10b   B(5)   18 m

The middle line which climbs to a bold, first bolt and then rides a horribly hollow flake to a small roof at 2/3 height. Beware the crux – pulling the lip on suspect flakes! Chain and hanger to lower. *Andrew Sauter, Gary Wolkoff '93*

3. Char-Broiled Baldness   5.9   B(3)   12 m

Right line which starts 4m from Gamelan. Fun, engaging climbing leads past 2 bolts down low, then eases off as you enter groundfall zone at the third clip. Hangers only. Dirty up top! *Mike Shannon, Lyle Thiede '97*

The next two climbs are about 50m right of the trail up to Toboggan Ledge. Climbs are on the south face, near the steep overhang. Exposure: south Routes: left to right.

4. Buckle Up **   5.6   Trad   22 m

The climb begins up the featured low-angle slab to a steep finish in the crack up top. A top-rope can be set up from Toboggan Ledge. This is a Kelowna classic and a very good beginner trad lead, with bomber cam placements. The rack : CDs up to 2" / nuts. Long slings are handy to rig the station (2 hangers). *Eric Rayson, Leon Blumer '60s*

5. Claw Hammer   5.10d   B(2)   6m

This is the 2-bolt boulder problem which starts with a left-trending feature and works its way over the lip. Lower from a single hanger. Scruffy at the crux. *Jeff Giebelhaus '93*

Scruffy Bluffs

The Scruffy Bluffs are the scruffy bluffs located at the eastern end of Cedar Park. This region has potential to develop as a beginner area because of the short routes and easy access to the top of the crags. Unfortunately, many of the original routes have hangers missing and stations stripped. Not much to see at press time.

Devil's Furnace

About 250 m (3minutes) east of Toboggan Ledge. Walk down the gully and look for the roof, just past some slab. Devil's Furnace was developed by Todd Guy and Mike Doyle in 1995. At press time, the crag was not ship-shape for climbing, suffering from stripped stations and hangers. Information is for reference only. Exposure: south   Routes: left to right.

The following three climbs all share the same start and go over the roof at different locations.

1. Skill And Frustration   5.12a   B (6)   12 m
Scramble up the slab, then traverse left along the roof. Crux over roof. No station. *Todd Guy, Mike Doyle '95*

2. Product of Imagination   5.12b   B(5)   8 m
Same start but traverse to halfway point of roof. Crux over the roof. No station. *Todd Guy '95*

3. Burning Cross
     5.11c   B (4)   8 m
Same start, but skip the traverse. Engage roof head-on. No station. Third bolt stripped. *Todd Guy '95*

The next 2 climbs once shared a station (stripped) and are just 3 metres right of Burning Cross.

4. Pissing Bliss
     5.11a   B (3)   6 m
Left line of bolts, just right of the arete. *Mike Doyle, Todd Guy '95*

5. Grounded
     5.11a   B (3)   6 m
Right line of stripped hangers. *Mike Doyle, Todd Guy '95*

(*right: Devil's Furnace photo; Jani*)

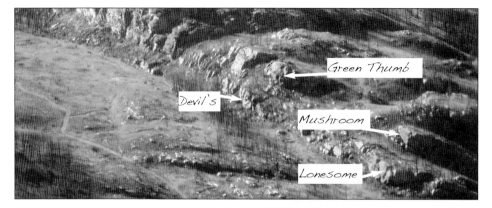

Green Thumb

Devil's

Mushroom

Lonesome

Green Thumb

Lonesome

1   2   3   4

Green Thumb Wall

Located 30m behind Devil's Furnace. Reach by scrambling up the slope 15m east of Devil's Furnace roof. This crag was developed by Anthony Comazzetto and John Mulligan in the mid-90s. There was a series of 5 or 6 climbs along this 10m high bluff, but at press time some hangers are gone and the 2 stations for the 3 climbs on the right are chopped.

Mushroom Buttress

Located 150m due east of Green Thumb Wall. Exposure: east

Graveyard Crow   5.9   B (4)   10 m
A line of bolts just right of an arete going up a short, chossy face. Chain station. Tyler set this up after a graveyard shift at work. *Tyler Parenteau '02*

Lonesome Ledge

Located 40m due east of Mushroom Buttress. This is farthest outcrop of rock at the eastern edge of Cedar Park, and can be accessed by Lair Trail. Walk east along the gully until it opens up into a meadow. Look for the old fence which intersects Lonesome Ledge on its right side (south).

Exposure: east   Routes: left to right

1. The Butler   5.10d   B (4)   10 m
Far left line of bolts, just right of the arete. Loose, chossy climbing all the way to the chains. *Dean Urness '98*

2. The Bachelor   5.10c   B (4)   10 m
Same start as the Butler, but move right up the loose, chossy face with suspect holds. Same station as last climb. *Dean Urness, Tyler Parenteau '99*

3. The Bachelorette   5.9   B (3)   8 m
Second line of bolts from the fence. A face climb on positive holds within the loose and chossy rock. Chains. *Tyler Parenteau '99*

4. The Best Man   5.9   B (3)   8 m
Far right line which starts beside the fence. Same loose and chossy rock to a chain station. *Tyler Parenteau, Dean Urness '99*

(aerial photo suppied by Mike Shannon)

The Lair is the newest crag at Cedar Park. Developed by locals Adam Tutte and Aaron Culver in 2007, the two discovered the Lair after climbing at Croissant Wall. Initially they had hoped to cut a trail from the west end of Cedar Park, but dead trees and steep terrain were an issue. They settled for expanding upon a deer trail around the back of the main crag.

From the parking lot head towards the main crag. At the fork in the trail, go right. This will take you along the far side of the Scruffy Bluffs, and over a cattle guard The trail heads down a fairly steep slope and veers left (west). The trail levels off as you walk along the back side of the main area, with a great view of Okanagan Lake on your right (north). After 15 minutes there is a small chossy crag. The trail veers right, up the slope, and then left at the top. Another 15 minutes of pleasant hiking through a field and then a burnt forest leads to yet another small crag. Five more minutes and there in front of you is the Lair.

The Lair is a work in progress and is in need of more cleaning. However, those making the 30-minute hike will enjoy the scenic journey as well as the climbs, as there is a good crag under the scruff.

above: Undeveloped south end of Lair. facing: Developed north end of the crag.

Ben Hardin working Itsy Bitsy Teenie Weenie.

①   ②   ③   ④   ⑤   ⑥

*above: Joanna Lige and
Karttika Culver cranking. left:
Aaron Culver and Ben Hardin
after
Ben pulled the FA on Itsy Bitsy
Teenie Weenie facing: Adam
Tutte pondering Burilious.*

The Lair

The east facing Lair offers climbs up to 25m high and generally steep (5 to 15° off vertical). It is a long wall, approximately 65m, with future routes planned for the undeveloped, chossy south end. The grades and stars were provided by Adam and Aaron and are subject to change. Some of the 5.12s have had only 1 or 2 ascents, and thus the grades will evolve.

Exposure: east   Routes: left to right.

1. Spank My Pink Panties **
                          5.9   B(6)   14 m
Farthest route to the left of the crag. This is a nicely bolted, off-vertical face climb which uses incuts and sidepulls to surmount the crux at midpoint. Rap hangers. *Adam Tutte '07*

2. Dangerous Beans ***
                          5.10b   B(6)   14 m
A natural flowing line which climbs up a right-leaning feature into a shallow dish. Trend left along the bulge to reach the station. Rap hangers. *Aaron Culver '07*

3. Itsy Bitsy Teenie Weenie *
                          5.12d   B(8)   25 m
Starts 3m left of the crack. A highly technical and very crimpy face leads to a big ledge 17m off the deck. Easier climbing on the upper headwall to the chains. Bolted by *Adam Tutte '07. FA Ben Hardin '07*

4. Balls To The Wall **
                          5.11b   Trad   25 m
Follow the obvious crack to about midheight on the crag. Crux through the face (good pro) and continue by following the broken crack to the station. Station same as Burilious. The rack : nuts / CDs to 3". *Adam Tutte '07*

5. Burilious ***   5.12c   B(11)   25 m
Start 5m to the right of the crack. Sustained climbing on slopers and pinches up to
the 15-metre mark. Switch gears to easier, crimpy face-climbing all the way to the
chains. *Adam Tutte '07*

6. Forbidden Fruit *   5.12c   B (8)   18 m
Another 5m right of Burilious. There is a distinct seam for the first 6m which involves
pinches and slopers and a wild deadpoint for your first rest. The crux is behind you,
but sustained climbing carries on 'til the chains. *Adam Tutte '07*

7. The Juggernaut *   5.12a   B (7)   18 m
Shares a start with the Grapes of Wrath, but heads slightly left after the second clip.
A long move off a dish-like sloper makes up the real meat of the route. Finish off on
a sustained face to the station. *Adam Tutte '07*

8. Grapes of Wrath ***   5.11c   B (7)   18 m
Starts 3m left of the arete, clip two bolts and then head right. A cool deadpoint gets
you established on the crimpy, upper face. Nicely sustained! *Adam Tutte '07*

9. Cutting Edge *   5.11c   B (7)   18 m
This is the obvious arete which arches right halfway up the wall. Ride the arete up
past the fourth bolt to the arch, then carry on up the face to finish. *Adam Tutte '07*

10. Project   18m
Aaron has a station right of the arete for a project. *Aaron Culver '07*

11. Enter The Dragon **   5.11b   B (6)   17 m
The line of bolts right of the corner. Climb on big holds up to a crimpy move below
the roof. Boulder over the roof on welcoming holds. Fixed station. *Aaron Culver '07*

12. Double Your Pleasure *   5.11b   B (8)   18 m
Open-handed climbing on big holds leads to a roof and a fixed draw. A crimpy boulder problem gets you over the short roof to a fixed station. *Adam Tutte, Aaron Culver '07*

13. Of Mice And Men ***   5.11b   B (5)   16 m
Farthest line to the right. Open-handed climbing on big friendly holds leads to a
right-facing corner / roof feature with a jug. Push and pull a bouldery sequence past
the roof to a fixed station. *Aaron Culver '07*

left: Karttika Culver approaching the crux, Dangerous Beans.

Janice McQuilkin climbing Attempted Theft in July (above) and
February (right). In February there was snow on the ground but
Lonely Boy was pretty dry! facing page: Lisa Armstrong belayed
by Don Debienne on One Eye Crack, Heli-pad (July). Note the
difference in attire for spring and summer climbing.

The Lonely Crags

The Lonely Crags are 5 minutes from Kelowna, and consist of 5 bluffs with climbs ranging from 8 to 20m. The jewel is Lonely Boy, featuring two classic routes (Lonely Boy 5.10d, State of Love and Trust 5.12a) that fall in the must-do category. Heli-pad and Lonely Boy are easy to top-rope, and offer up some challenging climbing for those not quite ready for stiff 5.10 leading. Lonely Girl is a great place for practicing easy 5.10 leading, and Lone Pine brings the lead bar up just a touch. The Lonely Crags are west facing; perfect for morning climbs on a hot, sunny day.

① ② ③ ④ ⑤

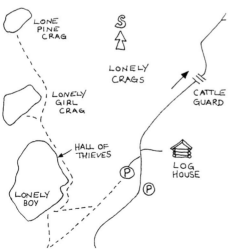

LONE PINE CRAG

S

LONELY CRAGS

LONELY GIRL CRAG

CATTLE GUARD

HALL OF THIEVES

Ⓟ

LOG HOUSE

Ⓟ

LONELY BOY

"Lonely Boy was just getting done - that's when I went over and had a look at Helipad. I've always liked to see lower end climbs go in 'cause I find that a crag that is all 11 and 12's is great but only those climbers will go there." JG

facing page: The ledge on Heli-pad. Jani is up front and that's Don Debienne in the background on Little Prana

Heli-pad

A 12m tall outcrop of rock with 5 routes. The face is visible on the drive in, and the top is visible from the trail, a mere 1 minute approach from the road. Scramble 2m up to the 'landing pad' if you are setting top-ropes. Long slings and locking biners will reduce drag, as these 4 stations are on the edge, and have hangers only. Little Prana is much safer to set up on lead.

Heli-pad's main draw is its easy access to top-ropes, short approach, and morning / evening cragging. On hot summer days it stays in the shade 'til noon. The jumbly path to the base of the crag is easy to find.

Exposure: west   Routes: left to right.

1. One Eye Crack *   5.9   Trad   12 m
On the left side of the crag is a crack with good pro but usually only gets top-rope ascents. Some hand jams and lots of face features. The angle lessens after the crux at midheight. The rack: nuts / CDs to 2". *Jeff Giebelhaus, Lee Smith '95*

2. One Eye Jack *   5.10d   B (4)   12 m
Start 1m. right of the crack. A stiff, balancy, side-pull crux gets you off the ground. After that, the climbing is more straightforward and a sustained 5.10 all the way to the top. *Jeff Giebelhaus, Lee Smith '95*

3. Fun Guy **   5.10b   B (4)   12 m
Scramble up a ramp and right to the first line of bolts. A nice climb with a series of cruxes at every bolt. You had better be good at mantles. Best line on the crag and well-bolted! *Jeff Giebelhaus, Todd Guy '95*

4. Not Lichen It   5.10b   B (4)   12 m
Scramble up the same ramp, but move to the line of bolts at the far right – just look for the rusty piton. Face climbing on less than positive holds. Hard-to-read crux awaits near the bulge. Seems a bit stiffer than Fun Guy. *Jeff Giebelhaus, Todd Guy '95*

5. Little Prana *   5.10c   B (3)   9 m
Far right side of the crag. Balance and footwork will get you up to the small roof/bulge feature. The holds here are good, but figuring a way through the crux will lead to a bit of a pump. Tricky and bouldery. Rap hangers. *Jeff Giebelhaus '95*

112

above: Jeff Giebelhaus relaxing on Tendonitis.

Lonely Boy

Lonely Boy and its panoramic views of Kelowna and Lake Okanagan make it an easy choice for cover art. The crag hosts 12 routes, most of which are high in quality. The rock is solid, and all of the climbs are challenging for the grade. Lonely Boy is best visited before noon during the summer months, while in the shoulder seasons it is a great afternoon crag. If you are in Kelowna and only have a few hours to crag, this is the place. It is a 20-minute drive from downtown and a 3-minute hike to the base of the crag.

Exposure: west   Routes: left to right

The first three routes share the same start.

1. Superfusion
                              5.12a   B (5)   10 m
This route starts 1m up and left from the main ledge. Climb up and trend left along the flaring crack feature. Face moves to exit. This sport climb features a bomber hand jam and a one-move-wonder crux. Rusty hook to lower from. *Todd Guy '96*

2. Mass Fusion *   5.11d   B (4)   10 m
Same start as last climb, but take the line of bolts which heads up the blank, steep wall. Great technical footwork and barely usable crimps make up this super stout 11d. The exit move is quite a charm as well. The name makes sense as you try to fuse your right hand to a crimp at the crux. Rusty hook to lower. *Todd Guy '96*

3. State Of Love And Trust ***   5.12a   B (4)   12 m
An absolute must-do Kelowna classic! Same start as Mass Fusion, but take the right hand line of bolts up the crimpy face. A cool deadpoint gets you through the first crux and an all-out-throw caps off this sustained boulder problem. Hooks to lower. *Todd Guy '94*

4. The Main Principle **   5.11c   B (6)   15 m
The red hangers which lead up to the bulge feature. Technical, sustained and cruxy. This route does not let up until the final mantle. Really good! Glue-ins to lower. *Todd Guy '94*

Lonely Boy cont.

5. Tendonitis **   5.11b   B (7)   15 m
This is another one of Jeff's many area classics. Start at a low bolt and head toward the dish. Step left and engage a sustained cruxy face to a welcome rest. A moderate mantle makes up the finale. Chains. *Jeff Giebelhaus '94*

6. Lonely Boy ***   5.10d   B (6)   17 m
This is the landmark climb of Kelowna, and dare we say the most climbed / attempted! Start at the right side of Todd's plaque and climb through to the right side of the dish. A cruxy move gets you through to the flake above and easier ground to the chains. *Gary Wolkoff, Andrew Sauter '91*

7. From Start To Finish *   5.11a   B (6)   17 m
Same start as Lonely Boy, but follow the finger flake out to the arete. Balancy, thin moves lead you up the arete to a final, reachy crux just before the top-out. Lower from Lonely Boy station. *Mike Doyle, Todd Guy '95*

8. Trads Are Us **   5.8   Trad   20 m
The right facing corner/crack system. Solid hand jams and stemming lead to the big, imposing roof. The roof is airy, but not the crux. Good fun. The rack: hexes / CDs to 2.5"/ a long, long sling. Chain station to lower. *Gary Wolkoff, Andrew Sauter '91*

9. Rumble Fish   5.10c   B (6)   15 m
This climb is on the face just right of Trads Are Us. Start by clipping in to protect the mantle move on to the large ledge. A crimpy hard-to-read crux just above the ledge leads to easier climbing and station. Don't feel bad if you miss this one. *Todd Guy '96*

10. Miss Carriage   5.10c   B (7)   18 m
Same style mantle and clip as Rumble Fish, then snake up the face. The reachy crux comes early, just as the ankle-breaking features below weigh on your mind. You've been warned! Chains up high. *Jeff Giebelhaus '97*

11. Aretenaphobia **   5.9   B (7)   18 m
John has a good eye for fun climbs. Just right of previous line is a ramp with a crack feature. A lovely, airy traverse along the arete, then merge with Miss Carriage for the finish. This has got to be the last addition to Lonely Crag. *John Lang, K. Hanna '06*

12. Attempted Theft *   5.7   B (4)   18 m
Around the corner from Aretenaphobia. Start in a corner and face climb up the wall on solid hand and foot holds. The station can be accessed for top-rope by scrambling up to the far right of the climb, or take the ramp near State of Love and Trust, and walk across the top. *Mike Ross '97*

Hall of Thieves

①　②

Lonely Girl

①　②　③　④　⑤

Hall of Thieves

This slabby, broken bluff is south facing and just around the corner from Lonely Boy. Routes: left to right

1. Spanish Girl *   5.10d   B (4)   7 m
Just left of the arete. A few tricky, technical moves make up the difficulty of this short line. Rap hangers. *Todd Guy '95*

2. The First Clip *   5.5   B (3)   7 m
Just right of Spanish Girl. Huge holds and huecos to the rap hanger station. Perhaps a nice climb for aspiring leaders. *Todd Guy '98*

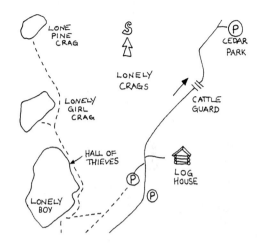

Lonely Girl

A 15m tall by 20m long crag with moderate climbs from 5.9 to 5.10c. Lonely Girl is a short walk from Lonely Boy. Follow the ridge line up a gentle slope and in 5 minutes you will be looking down at the base of Lonely Girl. Chains are located on the face and so are difficult to reach for setting up top-ropes. Much easier set on lead. Exposure: west Routes: left to right.

1. Lazy Boy *   5.10a   B (4)   12 m
Start at the far left side of crag. Some obvious direct moves lead to a more vertical section in the middle. Small holds and high feet get you to easy ground near the finish. *John Lang '00*

2. Bat Crap *   5.10c   B (3)   13 m
Second line of bolts and much the same as its neighbor to the left. Features a distinctly blank crux section thanks to the demise of a key hold. The route difficulty upped a couple degrees with this natural modification. Again, high feet does the trick. *Todd Guy, Curtis Guy '95*

3. Bat Slayer **   5.10a   B (7)   17 m
The longest line on the wall, crammed full of fun climbing. Start in front of an off-width crack with a big ledge above your head. A series of reaches to big holds leads to small but positive holds where the angle eases up. *Jeff Giebelhaus, Todd Guy '95*

4. Bat Girl *   5.10a   B (5)   15 m
A weaving line of climbing which uses vertical cracks and big positive holds. Trends slightly left up top to cross a slabby finish. *John Lang, Jeff Giebelhaus '00*

5. XXX **   5.9   B (6)   16 m
Another fun climb featuring a big, blocky line which is direct and obvious. Make sure you don't blow the last move to the chains! *Jeff Giebelhaus, John Lang '00*

Lone Pine

A short but solid crag which ranges in height from 7 to 10m. It is located about 5 minutes up a gentle slope behind Lonely Girl. Lone Pine was developed by John Lang and shows his enthusiasm for developing rock. The routes are short, with fun moves and above-average rock quality. Most of the stations can be accessed for top-roping. Trail around the back leads up the crag.

Exposure: west Routes: left to right.

1. Evolution *   5.11a   B (3)   7 m
Far left of crag. Climb up the steep slab to a bulge. A crimpy hold for the clip drains some energy before the crux, which is short-lived and followed by a slabby finish. *John Lang '06*

2. Project
John Lang has an unfinished line of studs up a stiff-looking bulge and blank face.

3. Scrubrats *   5.10c   B (4)   10 m
This is the line of bolts which swaggers up to and over the bulgy, broken seam. Make a cool move down low to gain some jugs, then swing left and follow the cracks to the top on a gentler angle. *John Lang '06*

4. Fuzzy Navel **   5.10c   B (4)   10 m
The original, and probably the best line on the wall. Same start as Scrubrats, but once you gain the jugs, make sequential moves out right and finish on some beauty crimps up the face. *John Lang '02*

5. Peter Piper *   5.10b   B (5)   9 m
Second line of bolts from the right. Fun, technical moves lead to the small, left-facing feature at midsection. Finish on the crimpy upper face. *John Lang '06*

6. Itsy Bitsy *   5.9   B (3)   8 m
This is the cool-looking arete at the right side of the crag, which starts on a face decorated with huecos. Lovely moves and friendly climbing. Could be a good first lead for a newbie. *John Lang, K.Hanna '06*

Huecos are not just the flavour of the day at Boucherie. Cedar Park boasts a few, as does Itsy Bitsy on Lone Pine. Hueco comes from the Spanish term for hollow, and in climbing refers to those big, solid pockets we love to pull.

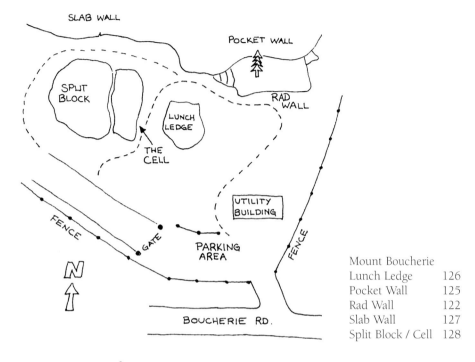

Mt. Boucherie

Mount Boucherie had a couple of trad routes / top-rope problems set up in the '60s by Leon Blumer, but all of its bolting occurred in the late '90s.

This unique outcrop of conglomerate rock is located close to town (Westbank is about 8 minutes, and Kelowna 15 minutes) and directly below the visible tower of Mission Hill winery. Climbing consists of easy to difficult technical slabs with pockets and crimps thrown in. There is one steep wall of 5.12 sport climbs (The Cell) and 3 beginner climbs for top-rope and rappelling. With its easy approach, southern exposure and lake level altitude, it is possible to climb Mount Boucherie every month of the year.

Nubbins come and go, but not so much during the long, dry summer. It is more of an issue after frost gets behind the rock, and then the sun warms things up. Pop! Keeps the routes interesting. For those people allergic to wasp bites, there are lots of them hanging out in the huecos pre-winter, when the males are being tossed from the swarm. However, they are sluggish, not aggressive, and fly off when a climber's hand enters their domain.

facing page: John Lang on Life's A Shopping Cart.

At a Glance: Approach: easy stroll, 1 minute Sun Exposure: All day / year-round
Rock: Conglomerate - nubbins and pockets Routes: 21 + 2 projects Grades: 5.6 to 5.12c
Style of Climbing: Sport - technical/steep top-ropes - easy slab / off-width chimney

Rad Wall

From the parking lot, take the hill trail just left of the utility building. Directly in front of you is Rad Wall.

Exposure: south Routes: left to right.

1. The Good *   5.9   B(4)   12 m
Left hand route which climbs up the face beside the arete. An engaging start lets you know that this is no cake walk, and that it's time to pay attention. *Jeff Giebelhaus '97*

2. The Rad **   5.10a   B (5)   15 m
Middle climb on the wall. A cruxy bit gets you going into a slabby dish at which point the route steepens. Nice features and fun stemming lead up to another lower angled section just below the chains. *Mike Ross '97*

3. The Ugly   5.9   B (4)   12 m
Right hand climb which ascends the scruffy, slabby face. It is rare to see someone on this one, but the name is a clue. *Jeff Giebelhaus '97*

"*I really like Boucherie. Best climbing I've ever seen on the shittiest rock I've ever seen. Some of the climbs are classics. It's a winter climbing area, no snow usually, no approach and if you are going to Smith - go there. The day before you go, go there and crank hard - then when you get to Smith you'll feel comfortable.*" JG

facing page: one of two meaty rappel loops on Slab Block installed for rescue training by the fire department / military.

Pocket Wall

Pocket Wall is directly above Rad Wall and has a lower and upper section.
Exposure: south   Routes: left to right.

1. Re-Vamp   5.10a   B (6)   22 m
Not exactly Jeff's showcase climb. Try following the bolts on the face and blunt arete
to the top of the crag. Nubbins mix with pockets and a bit of distance between bolts,
giving one either a great feeling of exposure, or a small bit of terror. Chains up top.
Jeff Giebelhaus '97

2. Pockets of Pleasure ***   5.10b   B (8)   22 m
This is an absolute must do when visiting Boucherie. Start left of an up and right
trending ramp in a slight concave. A devious hard-to-read crux makes you wonder
where are the pockets of pleasure. Nicely sustained and bolted. *Jeff Giebelhaus '97*

3. Pockets of Pain ***   5.11c   B (8)   18 m
Another Kelowna classic for those who enjoy sustained, technical face climbing.
Scramble 4m up and right from the base of last climb, clip the first hanger and it is
"on". The climbing stays sustained and steepens as you approach the chains. Save
some gas for the finale! *Todd Guy '97*

Upper Ledge
Scramble another 4m up and right from last climb. A rope tied to the tree on the ledge
helps the approach and descent.

4. Tales of Terror   5.11b   B(4)   13 m
Start just left of a small pine tree. This climb is very facey and the setter keeps you in
ground fall range all the way to the third clip. The name says it all. *Geoff Atkins '98*

5. Conglomerate Chaos **   5.10d   B (4)   13 m
Start immediately right of the tree. A nice face climb which uses pockets and nubbins
all the way up. The crux is very much on your feet. Nicely sustained! *Geoff Atkins, Jeff
Giebelhaus '98*

6. Volcanic Panic **   5.10b   B (4)   13 m
Start just left of a kooky detached column. Make a thin move up smooth slab to a
small overlap. Fun, friendly pocket-pulling up a nicely featured wall. Well worth the
scramble up the ledge. *Jeff Giebelhaus '98*

Lunch Ledge Slab is in front of Slab and Pocket, beside Split Block, and overlooks the vineyards and Okanagan Lake. It is a great place for lunch, and has one 5.6 route (18m) with a chain station for top-rope or rappel. Prevent rope drag by using long slings for the station. Set by Leon Blumer in the '60s.

facing page: Jani and John Lang on Conglomerate Chaos.

Slab Wall

Slab Wall is to the left of Pocket Wall and directly behind Split Block.
Exposure: south Routes: left to right.

1. Core *   5.8   B (2)   10 m
Farthest line to the left on a short, huecoed wall with a low angled slab on top. Move through on huge holds to a glue-in station. *Todd Guy' 95*

2. My Bud The Poser *   5.7   B (2)   10 m
Two metres right of core, another face with big huecos for climbing. Chain and biner for station. *Todd Guy '95*

The next climb is an extension of either of the first two.

3. Don't Let Friends Climb Slab
                5.6   B (4)   22 m
The low angled slab above the short pocketed
wall. There are four bolts and a chain station
that happens to be hard to see. *Todd Guy '95*

4. Life's A Shopping Cart **
                5.11c   B (3)   10 m
A highly technical climb which starts 2 metres
left of the crack. Bring your fancy footwork
and a solution for a move off a very shallow
mono pocket. *Todd Guy '96*

5. Tried To Be A Trad *
                5.10d   B (3)   10 m
The bolted crack. An engaging line which
leads into ground fall territory when you reach
the third bolt. (There is an upward flaring
placement for a nut which offers better pro for
the crux.) Glue-ins for the station. *Todd Guy '95*

6. Not Much
                5.10b   B (2)   8 m
Farthest line to the right, just 2 metres past the
bolted crack. Straightforward face climbing to
a thought-provoking sequence guarding the
station. *Todd Guy '95*

Split Block

Split Block's name comes from its cracked south face, but most climbers are attracted to the steep pocketed east face known as the Cell.

South Face

1. Split Block Slab   5.7   TR   25 m
Big old rings are set into the top of the Split Block for top-roping (bring long slings / webbing). Climb pocketed feature slab just left of the big chimney. *Leon Blumer '60s*

2. The Off-Width   5.6-ish   TR   25 m
Scramble up the ramp as for the slab then step right into the chimney and find the path of least resistance to the top. *Leon Blumer '60s*

Split Block - The Cell

Exposure: east Routes: left to right.

3. The Key *   5.12b   B (5)   16 m**
This is pocket pulling at its best in the Kelowna area. At the fourth bolt, move left for 1 more bolt and a bouldery crux. A key hold has been slowly deteriorating over the years, but it's still 12b and soooo good! *Todd Guy '97*

above: John Lang working the Key. right: Split Block, and its popular east face, the Cell.

4. Sentimental Argument ***   5.12c B (5) 16 m
Same start as The Key, but move right to a glue-in hanger and be ready to deal with a shallow mono which guards the chains. The crux is considered a V6 boulder problem, which probably ups the grade. *Todd Guy '97*

5. Mental Jail   5.12a B (5) 16 m
Right line of bolts. A bouldery sequence guards a good rail 3 metres above your head and that's just getting started. Dynamic movement and demanding clips highlight this benchmark 12a. If you're feeling strong you WILL dispatch the spoiler crux near the end. *Todd Guy '95*

John Lang has a project going on the far left of the Cell's steep wall, and Jani is working on a project immediately left of The Key.

130

" It takes a village to raise a child."
Margaret Mead, anthropologist

Here's another truth:
It takes a community to create a guidebook.

In this section we take you behind the scenes, and introduce you to some of the people and companies that are the backbone of Kelowna Rock.

Jani spoke with all the route setters we could find. They provided valuable information on past and future projects and are the reason we love climbing in Kelowna. Jeff Giebelhaus is the local king of route setting and has all kinds of interesting things to say in the next couple of pages. His quotes also appear here and there in the book under the sig JG. Wanna be a route setter? Jani provides advice to go with Jeff's words.

Our sponsors, most of whom are climbers, provided the much needed cash to pay the printers. We are grateful beyond words, and hope you will show your thanks by supporting these worthy companies. You support them, they support us, and you get a guidebook that is regularly updated. Win, win, win, really. Special thanks to the Alpine Club of Canada for their additional funding in support of alpine literature.

And then of course there is the gang of merry trail blazers. A lot of work goes into making our walls accessible, and these fellas simply get the job done, on their own time and dime. Leon Blumer, Eric Rayson, Jeff G., Mike Ross and James Cruikshank were some of the pioneer path finders, and guys like Mike Shannon, Jani, John, Rob Bannatyne and Craig Langford are carrying on their good work. We are all aware of the big access issues that surrounded Skaha Bluffs ($1 off every Kelowna Rock sold goes to The Land Conservatory Skaha Bluffs Access Fund), but it is important we also appreciate the micro-issues of keeping our trails maintained and accessible.

You play a role in keeping our climbing regions healthy by leaving the crags clean and removing debris from the trails. It is our own backyard, after all. If you have any comments or concerns or information regarding routes and walls and climbing in general, contact Hanna at bluemoo@telus.net.

Look forward to seeing you on the rock!

top to bot: Mike Shannon, Tom McLean, Kevin Easthope, Rob Bannatyne and Craig Langford, Mike Shannon (trail markers in his pack) Photos by April Smith, Jani and Hanna.

A dirty Jeff Giebelhaus after cleaning Route Canal on the Main Wall, Boulderfields.
Inset: Moments later, a shiny, clean Jeff.

The World According to Jeff

Jeff Giebelhaus has set more routes in the Kelowna area than any other living climber (his buddy Todd Guy beat him out by a dozen). His routes are favourites of most climbers, and many local setters (Jani and John Lang are two) will tell you that they learned a great deal of their art from Jeff. Jeff was the first guy bolting routes at the Boulderfields, created Heli-pad as a lower grade companion to Lonely Boy, and played a major role in the development of Mount Boucherie, Cedar Park and the Lonely Crags.

He began climbing at 19 by scrambling up routes in his runners, then bought a rope and learned to rappel. Jeff and I had a few discussions over java at Tim's, climbing at Lonely Boy and scrubbing routes at the Fields (Jeff scrubbed, I pestered). You will see his comments here and there throughout the book. Here's a sampling of the World According to Jeff.

In the Beginning
"
I saw a couple of old guys climbing Spiderman (Cedar Park). I was in awe. Back then (1980's) there was nobody (climbing). I had to drag whoever I could out there. They'd drink beer ... I'd teach them to belay and set up a top-rope. We climbed Spiderman, Lightning Roof (Chain Lightning), Alligator Breath, Noisy Oyster ..."

We had no quick draws. We had slings, cams and biners. Bolts were horrible. They were rivets banged in and so spaced out you could hit the ground anywhere you fell."

First bolted Route
"
My first route I bolted was Tendonitis (1994). I called it an 11a because it wasn't much harder than Lonely Boy, which we climbed so much it was pretty easy for us. Todd used to go solo on those routes. One day (on solo) he pulled off the (crux) hold on Tendonitis – he still managed to keep it together!"

The Generator
"
I didn't have a power drill (for Tendonitis) so I hauled in a generator ... (At Cedar Park) Marty really wanted to bolt this great line but he had no power drill - so he hauled in a generator and bolted it that way." *(see page 87, The Generator)*

Interesting Technique
"
I do good on hard climbs that have microholds that I can put my fingernails behind. I can reef on my fingernails. I let them grow a little bit long. I can hook them on things and I can pull like a bugger on them. My height and reach are good. I'm heavy. I'm weak. I don't have good balance or technique, but my reach has saved me a lot."

cont. page 135

Scary Route

" Edgefest (Main Wall, Boulderfields) It's scary, it's runout, but it's an easy climb. It's like a 5.6 but it just takes one mistake and you can take a 20-30 footer. And it isn't hard to fall. A foot hold snaps off and you're gone so quick you wouldn't know it."

Favourite Routes

" So many - Imp, Gravity Bites, Crack Addiction, Brutality, Relentless, Morning Stiffie, Natural Gas, Griptonite, Tendonitis – all the stuff on Croissant. That stuff's just great. Tons of good stuff. ... I like long steep climbs, the longer, the better. I'm not really into the short stuff."

Setting a Route / Grading

" Every time I go to a crag I look for the easiest lines first and that's what I set up. Around that you can look for the harder, better climbs. I've always liked to see lower grades go in. A crag that's all 11 and 12s is great but only those climbers will go in."

I try to set routes from the bottom up, climb it on TR and figure out my bolts. When it's an overhang, like Croissant Wall, you got no choice, you gotta bolt it from the top down."

A hard climb should be continuously hard, not a 5.7 with one 12d move on it. That to me is not a 12d. ... The harder you climb, the harder it is to grade routes. The easiest to grade are ones in your range."

The key to a good route?
The line of course, but lots of scrubbing." 鏡

Kelowna Route Setting Stats for Jeff

Cedar Park - 7 routes on 4 walls
Lonely Crags - 10 routes on 3 walls
Boulderfields - 29 routes on 17 walls
Mt. Boucherie - 5 routes on 2 walls

Want core strength and balance? John Lang has designed a really fun, free-standing 2.5m slack line for inside or outside, beginner or pro. For more info call John 250.469-4196.

Hauling up the drill for a project on the Cube.

The Complete Phrase Guide
for Belaying a Beginner

You got it.
Stay with it.
You look solid.
On your left.
By your knee.
Your other knee.
That's it.
I've got you.
You're fine.
It's a bit polished/thin/
wet/flaring/slopey/rattly/
wide/dirty/awkward,
but you got it.
It's just up a bit.
I'm with you.
Reach for it.
It's right there.

Bit more.
More.
Little more.
You can do it.
I'm right here.
You're doing great.
Just stand up on it.
I got you.
Move your feet up.
You're doing fine.
Shake it out.
Keep it going.
Don't give up.
You can make it.
I'm right here.
It's okay.
Calm down.

Trust your feet.
You're looking great.
It's on your right.
Your right.
Your other right.
Yep, I got you.
Stretch for it.
Little further.
Stay with it.
I've still got you.
Move your feet.
Keep it up.
You're almost there.
Don't give up now.
Uh-huh, I got you.
Really. I got you.
– repeat –

LEAVE PREPARED

MOUNTAIN EQUIPMENT CO-OP®

130 West Broadway, Vancouver | mec.ca | **ropes** | **harnesses** | **belaying devices**

Health & Fitness

Injury Prevention & Rehabilitation

Massage Therapy
Stott Pilates
Physiotherapy
Hand Therapy
IMS Treatment
Acupuncture

Premiere Massage Therapy Clinic
and Pilates Studio
Tel. (250) 860-4104   www.premierepilates.com

KELOWNA PHYSIOTHERAPY ASSOCIATES

Tel. (250) 860-2854
Fax (250) 860-2856
info@kelownaphysiotherapy.com

#205 3320 Richter Street, Kelowna, BC

So you want to put up a new route? by Jani Vaaranpaa

So you want to put up a new route? The first question you need to ask yourself is " Does the line inspire me?" If yes, then most likely others will want to climb it as well.

My goal is always to leave behind a route that I am proud of, that is safe, and that others will enjoy for years to come.

Some things to consider:

1. The Station – Getting down is just as important as getting up. The station should be set at a logical end to the climb, with the anchors mounted in solid rock, and positioned so the rope will run free of sharp edges.

2. Bolts - They need to be placed with great care and consideration. They too need to be mounted in solid rock, and so the clipping stance is comfortable for all heights. Allow the route to dictate where the bolts will go. Trying to force a line, or trying to get the climber 'to do something' is just annoying. If you are unsure consult others or top-rope first. Avoid squeeze plays, and drilling a hold should not be an option for obvious reasons.

Use stainless steel studs (minimum 3 inches long), stainless steel hangers and galvanized chains and quick links.

3. Cost - A 30-metre climb with 10 bolts and a rap station with chains costs about $70. The real cost is your time. Hanging in your harness and scrubbing is really hard work, and may take days. Just ask Jeff Giebelhaus, who has worn out more wire brushes, drill bits and ropes than anybody. Depending on rock quality, scrubbing one route can take 10 to 20 hours.

" Let see, my two drills – one was $800 and one was $450 and all the drill bits are $10-12 a piece. I spent $100 on hangers yesterday. A route costs anywhere from $20 to $100 a route plus all the time." Jeff G.

Clean away loose rock which could come off, as it could damage the rope or fall off and injure your belayer. Never expose a climber to a groundfall / ledgefall situation. If you have any doubts about what is good route setting, just go climb routes bolted by Jeff G. and Todd Guy. Those guys were craftsmen of the highest degree. 🏃

Let's not forget the role patient belayers like Brian Gibbons often play in setting a route.

Daniel Woods • Photo: Brian Solano

LA SPORTIVA®
innovation with passion
www.lasportiva.com

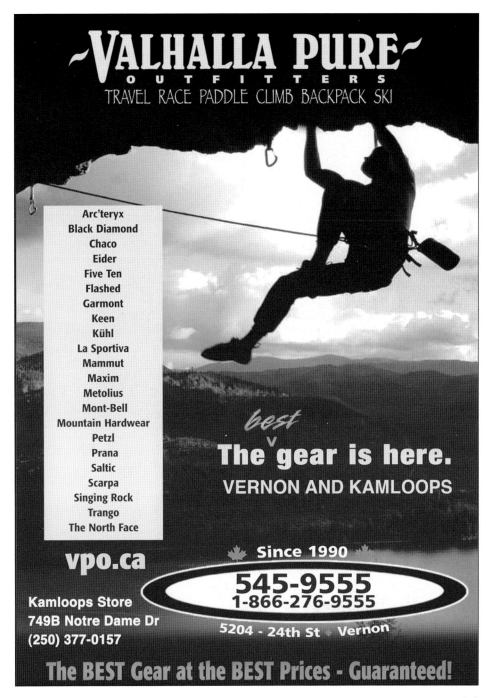

142

143

Association of Canadian
Mountain Guides Staff
Since 1993

Technical Rock Training
Top-Roping
Lead Climbing
Rock Rescue

Group Adventure Programs
Rock Climbing
Ropes Courses
Alpine Rock
Backpacking

Russ Turner, Director
www.skaharockclimbing.com
russ.turner@skaharockclimbing.com

250-493-1765

Kelowna Route / Problem Setters

THANK you Thank YOU thank you

Anthony Comazzetto	Jeff Giebelhaus
Aaron Culver	John Lang
Adam Gant	John Warren
Adam Tutte (2)	Ken Woodward
Barry Jones	Josh Mulligan
B. Labounty	Kirby Dunstan
Bud Godderies	Lee Sheppard
Chris Dunstan	Leon Blumer (3)
Chris De Vries (1)	Marty Zikmund
Craig Langford	Mike Doyle (5)
Dave MacPherson	Mike Ross
Dave Urness	Mike Shannon
Dean Urness	Nate Woods
Diane Doyle	Paul Gaucher
Eric Penninga	Rick Cox
Eric Rayson (4)	Ron Collins
Farley Klotz	Rob Bannatyne
G. Penninga	Scott Jeffries
Gary MacCallum	Terry Serhan
Gary Wolkoff	Todd Guy
Geoff Atkins	Tom Freebairn
James Cruikshank	Tyler Parenteau
Jani Vaaranpaa	Vic Kramer

(1)

(2) (3)

(5)

(4)

BEYOND THE CRUX
CLIMBING GYM
www.beyondthecrux.com
#2 1414 Hunter Court
Kelowna
250.860.PEAK (7325)

"BEST
BOULDER CAVE
IN THE WORLD!"
MIKE DOYLE

BTC

148

TR indicates there are routes on the wall that can be top-roped.

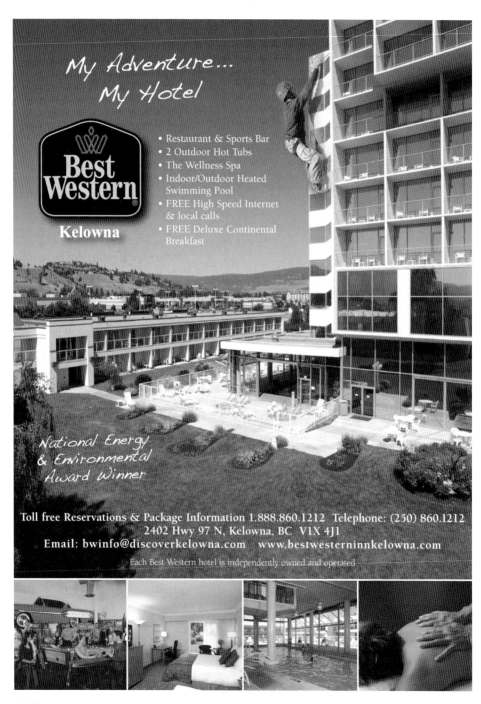

My Adventure...
My Hotel

Best Western
Kelowna

- Restaurant & Sports Bar
- 2 Outdoor Hot Tubs
- The Wellness Spa
- Indoor/Outdoor Heated Swimming Pool
- FREE High Speed Internet & local calls
- FREE Deluxe Continental Breakfast

National Energy & Environmental Award Winner

Toll free Reservations & Package Information 1.888.860.1212 Telephone: (250) 860.1212
2402 Hwy 97 N, Kelowna, BC V1X 4J1
Email: bwinfo@discoverkelowna.com   www.bestwesterninnkelowna.com

Each Best Western hotel is independently owned and operated

TR indicates there are routes on the wall that can be top-roped.

TR indicates there are routes on the wall that can be top-roped.